A Place in Ti

Britain 1450–1700

Rosemary Kelly

Stanley Thornes (Publishers) Ltd

This book is for my grandchildren, Polly, Matthew and Ben.

First published in 1990 by:
Stanley Thornes (Publishers) Ltd
Old Station Drive
Leckhampton
CHELTENHAM GL53 0DN
England

British Library Cataloguing in Publication Data

Kelly, Rosemary
    A place in time: Britain 1450–1700
    1. Great Britain, history
    I. Title
    941

    ISBN 0–7487–0029–3

Typeset by Tech-Set, Gateshead, Tyne & Wear.
Printed and bound in Great Britain at The Bath Press, Avon.

*The picture on the **cover** is part of a very unusual portrait painted in the time of Queen Elizabeth I. It tells the life story of an Elizabethan gentleman called Sir Henry Unton. In the bottom right-hand corner, Sir Henry is a baby in his mother's arms. You can find out quite a lot about rooms in big Elizabethan houses by looking carefully at this scene. Above, Sir Henry is about 17 and a student at Oxford University. It is easy to see who he is, because he is bigger than everyone else.*

Sir Henry was a rich landowner, and the artist has painted his house too – like a doll's house, with one side cut away so you can see inside. In an upstairs room Sir Henry sits reading. In the main room, Sir Henry and his wife are giving a party. They are bigger than the guests sitting round the table, so it is easy to pick them out. (They were not really bigger of course.

Why did the artist do this?) The guests each have their own knives and no one uses forks.

There is an entertainment called a masque going on. The actors are dressed up as Greek gods and goddesses, and recite and sing. The orchestra is playing several kinds of musical instrument.

There are more scenes from Sir Henry's life in the rest of the picture. It gives us all kinds of evidence about Elizabethan life. It hangs in the National Portrait Gallery in London.

*The picture on the **title page** is a portrait of Queen Elizabeth I, painted in 1590 when she was almost 60. The artist, Marcus Gheeraedts, has painted a stormy and a sunny sky, and Queen stands on a map of England. What does the picture tell you about Elizabeth I?*

Contents

Year	Monarch	Event
1450	Henry VI	
60		The Wars of the Roses
	Edward IV	
70		
	Edward IV	Caxton's printing press
80		
	Richard III	The Princes in the Tower disappear ✂ Bosworth
90		Columbus reached the Caribbean
1500	Henry VII	
		Leonardo painted *Virgin of the Rocks*
10		✂ Flodden
		Wolsey became Chancellor
		Luther challenged the Pope
20		
30	Henry VIII	
		The break with Rome
		The dissolution of the monasteries
40		
		The *Mary Rose* sank
50	Edward VI	
	Mary I	Protestant martyrs
60		
70	Elizabeth I	1542–1605 Akbar ruled the Mughal Empire in India
80		
		Execution of Mary, Queen of Scots
		The Spanish Armada
90		
1600		Poor Law
		East India Company founded

Year	Monarch	Event
1600		
	James I	Gunpowder Plot
10		Galileo's first telescope
20		*Mayflower* sailed to New England
		11 years without Parliament began
30		
	Charles I	
40		Long Parliament
		Civil War began
		Execution of Charles I
50	Protector Cromwell	✂ Worcester
		Cromwell died
60		The Great Plague
		The Great Fire
70	Charles II	
80		
	James II	The Revolution of 1688
90	William and Mary	✂ of the Boyne
1700		

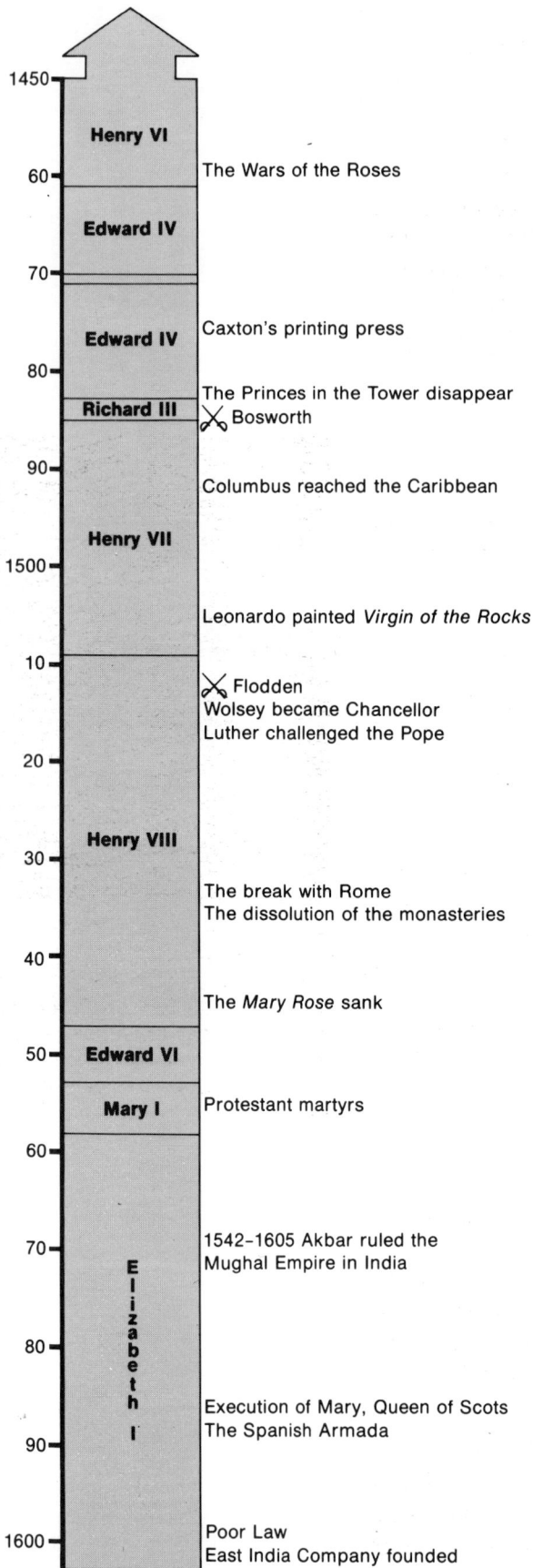

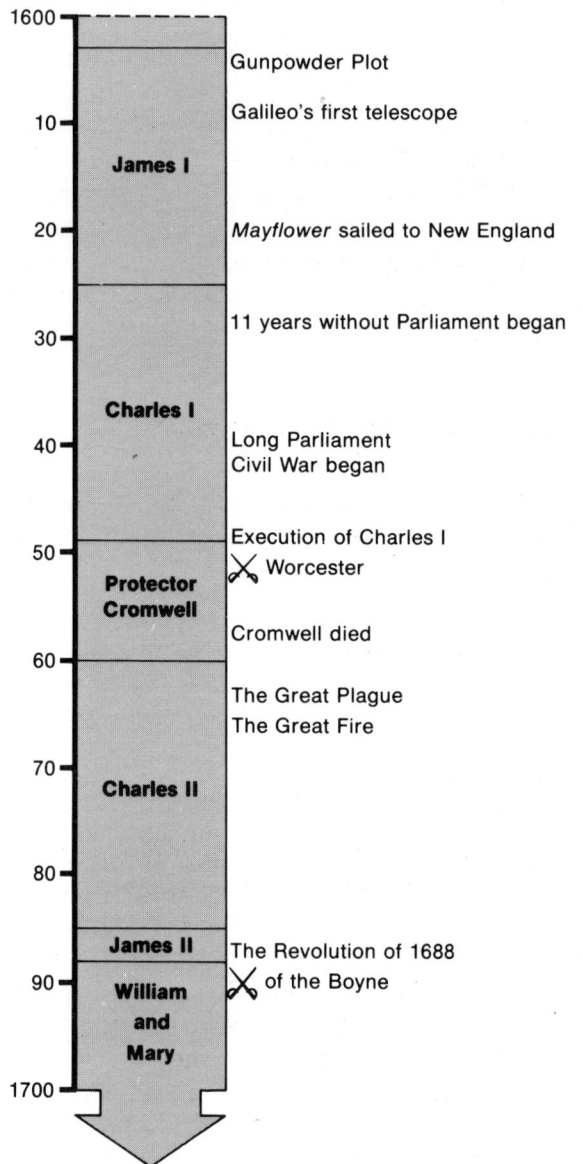

Timeline of some important events in the Early Modern Age.

A place in time

History is the story of past times. When you study History you discover many different places in time. This book is about one of them – Britain from 1450 to 1700. We sometimes call this time the Early Modern Age, because there were so many changes then which are still important in our modern times. On the back cover is a timeline which shows the labels we use for all the main times in History.

Discovering the past

It is not always easy to discover what it was like to live in places in time which are different from our own. We need several **tools** to do it.

Tool 1: Evidence

Evidence about the past comes from many different kinds of sources.

Written evidence Government records, letters, diaries and so on.

Pictures This book is full of paintings and engravings (printed drawings) which were all done at the time, and give us a great deal of information about the people and events they show. There are modern photographs too, of objects and buildings which have survived from the past, and help us to understand it. It is even better if you can manage to see some of these for yourself.

Places If you can visit any of the places connected with people and events in this book, you often find out more about them. Maps help too.

Tool 2: Historical imagination

This is also sometimes called **empathy**. It means trying our best to understand what it was like to live in times very different from our own, when people often had different attitudes and opinions from us. For instance we find many of the cures used by doctors in the Early Modern Age very extraordinary (see pages 18–21), but sensible people at the time believed in them. We have to understand why.

We must be careful about this word 'people' too. Rich courtiers, poor villagers, women of different classes, and children all led different kinds of lives and did not necessarily all feel the same way. We do not always know how they felt; and it is usually easier to find more evidence about richer people; and more about men than women. Can you think why?

One kind of evidence: some of the objects recovered from the medicine chest belonging to the surgeon on board the Mary Rose, a Tudor warship which capsized and sank in 1545. In front there is a half empty jar of ointment and a syringe (see pages 42–3).

You can probably see that Tool 2 is sometimes difficult to use, but it is also a very important one.

Tool 3: Organisation

We have to organise what we find out. We must put events in the right order, decide which we think are the most important and explain them clearly. Both drawing and writing can help here.

Tool 4: Understanding

Finally we have to try to understand the 'place in time' in this book, especially:

Causes   Why events happened as they did.
Results   The effect events had on people's lives.
Change   What changes happened.
Continuity   What stayed the same.

How to use this book

There are plenty of sources in this book which give you evidence about this 'place in time'. But remember that in any book like this, there is not enough space for *all* the evidence, and the author has to select what seems most important. There is almost always more to find out.

Written sources can be exciting and interesting, but old-fashioned language is sometimes difficult to understand, and people did not bother much about spelling. In this book we have used modern spelling.

Three dots like this . . . means we have left out something which we felt was less important.

[Words in brackets like this] mean we have used modern English to make it easier to understand.

There are **questions** to help you use the four Tools. They have the number of each Tool by them like this to remind you which Tool you are using.

Flashback signs like this ◄ 22 refer to pages earlier in the book. They help you to use Tools 3 and 4 by linking up information you have already read about with new facts and ideas.

Key words at the end of each chapter will help you use Tool 4.

Testing the evidence

When you read descriptions written at the time, always remember that however old they are, real people wrote them. These people had their own opinions, feelings and experiences. They were writing at a particular time and in a particular place. If their

---

Money

In old money:
20 shillings = £1
1 shilling (1s) = 12 old pennies
(12 d).

The value of money was nothing like it is now, so it is no good trying to turn these sums into modern money. But this is a useful guide to remember:

> In Tudor times, the average daily wage for an ordinary labourer was about 5 old pence. By the seventeenth century it was about 1 shilling. It cost a Tudor nobleman at least £1000 a year to run his household.

Look back at this box when money sums are mentioned.

evidence is going to be useful to you, you must always ask yourself three questions: **who? when? where?** – even if you cannot always find all the answers.

Look at this description of what English people ate. What answers are there to the three questions?

> They eat very frequently, at times more than is suitable, and are particularly fond of young swans, rabbits, deer, and seabirds. They often eat mutton and beef. They have all kinds of fish in plenty and great quantities of oysters.

Who wrote it?   An Italian visiting England. We do not know much about him, but he must have been rich enough to travel, and educated enough to write a description like this.
When?   In 1500.
Where?   We do not know for sure, but he also describes London, so he probably went there – but perhaps no further.

So there is a lot we do not know about this Italian visitor. We can guess he was talking about the rich people like himself whom he met in London. His description does not tell us about the meals of a nobleman in Scotland, or what a poor person could afford to eat. It is a one-sided view. We call it biased evidence.

It is still useful. We learn that some rich English people ate more meat than was good for them, and what a foreign visitor thought about it. We can work out a little about this visitor too.

Now read the list in the margin (notice the date). Then look carefully at the picture of people preparing a banquet in the kitchen of a great house in the sixteenth century. Does this evidence agree with what the Italian visitor said in 1500? What can you learn about eating habits in the sixteenth century?

In 1558, the Earl of Shrewsbury's household (probably about 150 people) ate and drank in Christmas week:

  3 quarters (38 kg) of wheat
  12 sheep
  26 hens
  10 capons (large chickens)
  118 rabbits
  441 gallons (1764 litres) of beer
  6 geese
  7 cygnets (young swans)
  1 turkey
  7 pigs

You have looked at three pieces of **primary evidence**. This means they were written or painted at the time. Historians have to look at (and test) as much primary evidence as possible to try to find out what really happened.

History books *use* primary evidence, but the books themselves are usually written long after the time they describe. They are **secondary evidence**. This book is secondary evidence.

A Fete at Bermondsey by J. Hoefnagel, painted about 1571.

1 Living in the Early Modern Age

What do you think is happening in the picture opposite? No one is quite sure. People used to think it was a picture of a wedding, but it may be a village festival. There is obviously a lot of merry-making going on. The fiddlers are playing away for the dancers in the centre, and behind them servants bring huge pies for everyone to eat. A serious looking group are coming from the church, and in the background on the left some grandly dressed visitors are arriving.

We know this picture was painted when Elizabeth I ruled England, and that it shows the village of Bermondsey, near London. That gives us our first clue about living in the Early Modern Age. Bermondsey is now in the middle of London. But then it was right in the country. Nine out of every ten people lived in the country. Towns were very small compared to modern ones. London seemed huge to the people of that time, but there were only about 60 000 people living there in 1500. Now there are about 6 million.

Knowing your place

In the Early Modern Age people believed God had put them in their place in the world. William Harrison, a clergyman who lived in Elizabeth I's reign, wrote a description of England in his time. He said:

> We in England divide our people commonly into four sorts, as gentlemen, citizens . . ., yeoman, and . . . labourers.

The artist who painted the picture opposite perhaps wanted to show the different social classes. He may have put himself in – the man in black standing behind the fiddlers, watching the whole scene, and looking a bit superior.

Gentlemen were the *First Sort*, the top people. The people wearing black, and coming out of the church, probably live in the big house in the village. They own most of the land. They do not do their own cooking and cleaning, nor work in the fields, so they employ most of the other people in the picture. But the grandest of the First Sort were noblemen, who owned several great houses and huge amounts of land. They were the most important people in the areas where they lived. They spent a lot of time at court in London – or wherever the Queen was. They dressed in the height of fashion in silks, velvets, furs and soft leather. They owned fine horses, and enjoyed hunting and jousting (see page 40). Perhaps the people arriving on the left of the picture are nobles from the court.

The *Second Sort* – citizens – often lived in towns. They were prosperous merchants or craftsmen. Or they might have a special skill which made it easy to earn a good living. The musicians in the picture are well dressed. They are probably a travelling group, who are good at their job, and doing well.

Yeomen – the *Third Sort* – did quite well too. They owned small farms or rented them from the local landowner, and were able to grow enough food for themselves, with some left over which they could sell. William Harrison tells us some could afford luxuries like feather pillows on their beds. In the old days, he said, they just put a log under their heads at night.

The *Fourth Sort* were everyone else – most of the people in England. They were labourers, servants and other wage-earners in country and town – mostly in the country. They could be very poor.

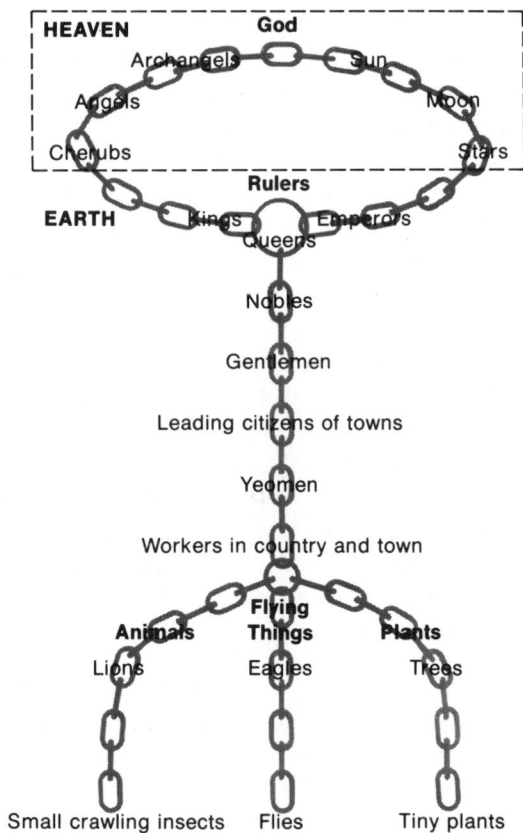

The idea that everyone had their place was part of a bigger idea – that all creatures in heaven and earth from God to the tiniest fly or beetle were linked together in a 'Great Chain of Being'. It was supposed to work something like this.

HEAVEN
God
Archangels — Sun
Angels — Moon
Cherubs — Stars

EARTH
Rulers
Kings — Emperors
Queens
Nobles
Gentlemen
Leading citizens of towns
Yeomen
Workers in country and town

Animals — Flying Things — Plants
Lions — Eagles — Trees
Small crawling insects — Flies — Tiny plants

1 Find people in the picture of the festival in Bermondsey who you think belong to the Third and Fourth Sorts. Choose two from each Sort, and explain your choice. You could also do small sketches of them.

2 Make your own diagram of the Great Chain of Being. Use a whole page, and plenty of coloured illustrations. You could add extra groups of animals, flying things and plants.

Going up in the world

The divisions between people in the Early Modern Age sound very firm and organised. But life is not always like that. Of course energetic people who wanted to do better sometimes went up in the world – and people who were lazy, or spent too much money, could do badly.

More than a hundred years before the Bermondsey picture was painted, a farm labourer called Clement lived in a tiny village called Paston in Norfolk. He took his surname from his village. This is how a neighbour described him:

> A good plain *husbandman* [labourer] and lived on the land he had in Paston ... he rode to the mill on bare horseback with his corn under him, and brought back *meal* [flour] ... and drove his cart with corn to sell as a good husbandman should. ... Clement had a son William which he sent to school ... and after that he learned the law ... and he purchased much land in Paston.

Going to school, becoming a lawyer and buying more land helped William Paston to go up in the world. Two other things helped too. William made a good marriage which brought him more land, and he made friends with an important local landowner, Sir John Fastolf. The Pastons continued to do well. Fifty years later they were one of the most important families in Norfolk. They owned a lot of land and several houses. The head of the family, John Paston, was a friend of the Earl of Oxford, one of the King's leading councillors.

1 Which Sort did Clement Paston belong to? Which Sort did John belong to? What evidence do you have for your conclusions?

2 Copy the diagram below. It shows two of the steps which the Paston family took to go up in the world. Fill in the rest of the steps in a sensible order, to show everything which helped the Pastons to become rich and important. You can add more steps if you need them.

3 We know a lot about the Paston family because they were great letter writers, and many of their letters to each other have survived. Some are used in this chapter. You may be able to find out more about the Pastons in your local library.

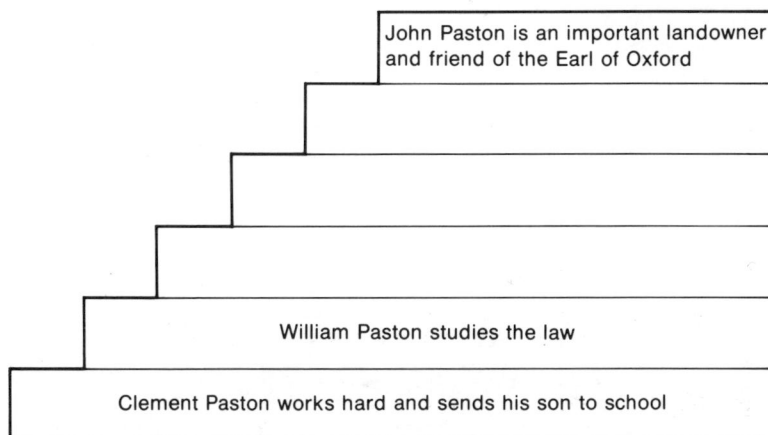

John Paston is an important landowner and friend of the Earl of Oxford

William Paston studies the law

Clement Paston works hard and sends his son to school

The Pastons go up in the world

A woman churning butter. Making butter and cheese was one of women's many everyday tasks in the house.

Women's lives

You may have noticed that the pages you have read have been about men in the Early Modern Age, and so far women have not been mentioned. But at least half the people in the Bermondsey picture are women – and so was at least half the population of England!

However, women had little chance to be independent. A girl was completely under her father's control until she married, and then she was expected to obey her husband. Her education prepared her to be a wife and mother. Her parents arranged her marriage for her. A marriage was a business arrangement, and both families would expect to gain from it. Brides had to bring a dowry with them. This was a sum of money, and often some land as well (remember William Paston). Even an ordinary farm labourer would hope to gain some strips of ploughland or a few cows when he married.

In 1477, Margery Brews sent a Valentine to the man she wanted to marry – John Paston. She said that if John will be content with a dowry of £100 and 50 marks,

> I should be the merriest maid on earth ... good true and loving Valentine.

But she was worried because her father could not pay any more. If he had to, he would not have been able to afford dowries for her sisters. This couple's problems worked out. They were married a few months later – and Margery's letter sounds as if they were in love, too. Arranged marriages were not always happy, but couples often grew to love each other.

If a girl did not get married, there was not much else she could do. She could become a nun – but not everyone wanted to do that. Otherwise she stayed at home or lived with her married sisters, often like a servant. The nickname 'spinster' for an unmarried woman was not very kind. Spinning was boring work, which was often left to her.

Women worked in the fields alongside men, especially at busy times like haymaking. But not everyone seems to be working here!

Once a girl was married, her husband controlled her life and everything she owned. She worked hard. Look at the pictures on these pages and the evidence below.

Advice to the housewife

This comes from a book of advice to farmers written in the sixteenth century. It tells the housewife how to organise her day, which should always start with a prayer:

> And when *thou* [you] art up and ready, first sweep *thy* [your] house . . . and set all things in good order: milk thy *kine* [cows] . . . take up thy children and *array* [dress] them, and provide for thy husband's breakfast, dinner and supper, and for thy children and servants . . . take corn and malt to the mill to bake and brew . . . Thou must make butter and cheese . . . [look after] thy pigs and poultry . . . and in the beginning of March it is time for the housewife to make her garden, and to get as many good seeds and herbs for the pot and to eat . . . let thy *distaff* [a stick used to hold wool when spinning] be always ready that thou be not idle . . .

It certainly does not sound as if there is much time to be idle. But the author has not finished yet. A wife has to grow flax to make linen sheets, and hemp (she used its seed for medicines, and the tough fibre stalks for ropes). She must also go to market. Husbands and wives must share the money they make and not cheat each other. And a wife must help her husband 'fill the dungcart, drive the plough . . . and load hay and corn.'

1 How can you tell that this advice was written for fairly well-off people?

2 Make a list of the things this housewife has to produce or grow, which today she could buy in the shops.

3 Look at the picture above. We do not know who these people are. The man could be a farmer just back from market. His wife has not had time to go, because she had to help with the haymaking (as in the picture opposite). She has been very rushed, and the supper is burnt. Write the conversation between husband and wife – and make sure the wife tells her husband all about her day.

Sometimes, if a woman's husband died, she might become quite independent. This was often true in towns. A rich merchant's widow might go on running his business. Alice Chester of Bristol continued her husband's trade, importing iron from Spain, after he died. She did so well that she gave a beautiful carved screen to a church in Bristol, and a huge loading crane for the city docks.

A widow could also often decide for herself to marry again. If she was rich she was a good catch, so she could make a good bargain for herself. But it all depended on luck. Most women had no independence, and could not choose how to run their lives.

Alice Chester's crane in Bristol may have been like this one in Bruges in the Netherlands, which was the first of its kind. How is the power provided to lift the heavy barrels?

A woman cooking on her open fire.

Children

This picture shows William Brooke, Lord Cobham, and his family in 1567. Lord Cobham is keeping a firm eye on everyone. His wife Frances sits beside him with one-year-old Henry on her lap. Her unmarried sister Jane stands in the background. The artist has put the ages of the children, but it is difficult to see unless you can look at the actual picture in Longleat House. This chart shows them in order of age:

WILLIAM = FRANCES

William	Elizabeth and Frances	Margaret	Maximilian	Henry
6	twins of 5	4	2	1

1 Find the children in the picture. How has the artist made it easy to find William? Why is he the most important child?

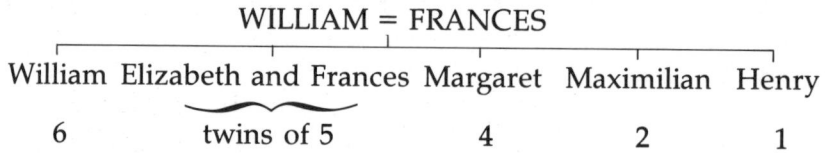

2 Make a list of as many things as you can which show that this is a rich and important family. You can start with the fact that they can afford to have a big portrait like this painted.

This family is lucky as well as rich. People had bigger families in the Early Modern Age than they do now – but more children died young. Many parents lost at least half their children before they were five. But the six Cobham children are close in age – there are no sad gaps in this family. (Their mother Frances was still only 25 – rich girls usually married young.)

Babies and toddlers

After the new baby's first bath, the midwife would wrap its body in tight bandages called swaddling bands, so that it looked like a little parcel. This was convenient – babies could be hung up like parcels wherever it was easy to keep an eye on them. Swaddling bands were supposed to protect them from draughts, and make their limbs grow straight – but there must have been many cross uncomfortable babies.

Rich toddlers of both sexes usually wore long white dresses. When they were about five, they were dressed like miniature adults. (Look at the Cobham children, even the toddlers.)

We cannot answer question 4 definitely. We can however be sure of one thing: rich children did not have clothes which were easy to wear and to wash, like modern children's clothes. They wore layers of stiff heavy materials – often expensive silk and velvet.

So this helps us to understand how children were expected to behave. A good child was 'gentle, meek and kind', said a sixteenth century book of advice for children. They must be very respectful to their parents. There was trouble if children were disobedient, noisy or cheeky. Parents were much stricter than now and beating was a common punishment. Perhaps it was not always as bad as it sounds – Sir Thomas More (page 48) seems only to have beaten his children in fun with a peacock feather.

Getting dressed for this 4-year-old girl was a very complicated affair. She wears a bodice stiffened with whalebone and a starched ruff. Her padded sleeves are separate from the dress and are tied on with laces. Underneath she has several layers of petticoats, and stockings tied at the knee with ribbon.

This sixteenth-century picture shows us a scene just after the birth of a baby.

1 Describe what all the people in the picture are doing.

2 Find evidence in the picture which helps to explain why mothers and babies were so much more likely to die in the sixteenth century than they are now.

Our best evidence for children's clothes comes from portraits. But think about these questions:

3 What kind of children would never have their portraits painted?

4 Does what a child wears in a portrait really give us evidence for what he or she usually wore? (What might you wear for an extra special photograph?)

5 Describe what might happen as the mother of the little girl shown on this page dresses her, so she is ready for her portrait to be painted.

11

Boys and girls from very rich families

They often went to live in other rich households when they were about seven. Tutors gave them lessons and they learnt how to behave on grand social occasions.

Girls from less important families

They usually stayed at home. Their mothers taught them how to run a house – and sometimes to read (if they could read themselves). There were very few girls' schools.

Apprentices

Boys (and some girls) aged seven went to live with a shopkeeper or craftsmen to work for their master and learn a trade. Their families had to pay to send them.

Poor children in country and town

They worked hard for their parents as soon as they were old enough – in the fields, at home or in the shop.

Going to school

Today we take it for granted that everyone goes to school. This was not true in the Early Modern Age. Look at the diagram.

The number of schools increased during the Early Modern Age and so more children were able to go to school. Most of these new schools were 'grammar schools' in towns. Some of these schools were free, so quite poor boys could go to them. The pupils worked very long hours, and learned a great deal of Latin grammar. The picture of the sixteenth century grammar schoolroom below shows there are three classes in the same room. How noisy do you think it was?

1 Find as much equipment as you can in this picture. What object can you see which is also in the box on reading and writing opposite? How much furniture is there?

2 The teachers are obviously very strict. How do they keep order? What do you think will happen to the boys reading aloud to the teacher in the front of the picture, if they make a mistake? What clues can you find on the page opposite which tell you other reasons why children could be punished?

3 Use all the information on these two pages to write a story in which you are taken back in time to the sixteenth century. (If you are a girl, I am afraid you will have to turn into a boy!) Describe a day at a grammar school and how you feel about it. Do not forget to include the kind of equipment you use, and how you are expected to behave. You can also use the beating incident on the left of the picture of the school. Are you going to be the victim? What have you done to get the beating?

Learning to read and write

A lot of children never learnt to read and write. If they came from quite well-off families, they often learnt at home, before they went to school.

Children learnt to read from a horn book – a piece of wood protected by a layer of transparent horn. They had to learn the alphabet and the Lord's Prayer by heart. This kind of writing is called 'secretary hand' – it is not easy to read. A double 's' looks like an 'f'.

Pen knife to trim the point of the quill when it became soft.

Ink bottle (to hold the ink) with stopper.

Quill pen – the feathers were trimmed off. Each pupil had a 'penner' (a sheaf of quills).

Learning to write was difficult and messy. A child had to learn to use this equipment straightaway – and there were punishments for blots. A schoolboy took his own writing equipment and candles to school.

1 Make your own horn book. Use a piece of card approximately A4 size, and try to copy the writing as well as you can. Cover it with plastic film. If you are very ambitious, you could try writing it with a quill.

2 Make lists in two columns to show the differences in learning to read and write in the sixteenth and in the twentieth century. (Think about how you learnt to read and write, and the books and equipment you used).

3 Think of reasons why a lot of children never learnt to read and write. Look at 'Children who did not go to school' opposite. Which children do you think had
a) almost no chance to learn to read and write?
b) less chance than most?
(Would their parents be able to read and write? What kind of work would they expect to do when they were grown up?)

A grammar schoolboy's day

6.00 a.m.	Get up. Breakfast of bread and watered beer. Walk to school with books and equipment.
7.00 a.m.	School begins with prayers. Questions about last Sunday's sermon. Repeating Latin sentences by heart.
11.00 a.m.	Dinner. Beef, bread, watered beer. Time to play – football, skittles perhaps.
1.00 p.m.	Lessons begin again. Writing Latin sentences, and an essay in Latin. Religion.
3.30 p.m.	Short break.
3.45 p.m.	Lessons again.
4.50 p.m.	Prayers and Bible reading.
5.00 p.m.	Go home. There are a lot of Latin sentences to learn for tomorrow.

A Latin lesson

In Latin lessons, pupils usually repeated sentences learnt by heart, or wrote out sentences like these, from a sixteenth century textbook. They were in Latin. A child had to translate them into English – and was supposed to learn good behaviour as well:

Get up in good time
Make your bed neatly
Say your prayers
Clean your shoes
Brush your clothes
Comb your hair
Wash your hands and face
Do not pare your nails at table
Do not pick your teeth with a knife
Do not drink your soup too loudly and do not blow on it to cool it
Do not cram your mouth or plate too full
Do not lean your elbows on the table and stare about
Eat what is put before you

13

Country people

Houses

Ordinary people in the country had hard lives. Think what it must have been like living in the house in the picture below in bitter winter weather.

Lighting and heating   Everyone needed a fire for cooking, and to provide heat and even a little light. It was a disaster if the fire went out in weather like this, and people had to work hard to gather enough wood to keep it going. At night the old woman who lived in this house would damp it down with turf. In times of trouble, this had to be done at a certain time, after which everyone had to stay indoors. This was a curfew, which probably comes from *couvre-feu*, French for 'cover the fire'.

Candles were a luxury which ordinary people usually could not afford. Wax candles were very expensive. Candles made from tallow (animal fat) were more common – and smellier. But animals were thinner in those days, especially during the winter, so tallow could be expensive too. Most people managed with a rushlight. This was a reed or a stick soaked in any waste fat they might have and fixed in a stand. They were smoky, smelly and gave very little light. So people did not sit around much on dark cold evenings. They went to bed at dusk and started work when it was light.

Even in the daytime this house was very dark. Glass became cheaper in the sixteenth century, but it was still too expensive for people who lived in a house like this. So windows were small. People put pieces of horn or oiled linen across them to keep out rain and snow. Of course this also kept out the light. But at least by the sixteenth century a house like this had a chimney, so smoke from the fire could escape without filling the room first.

Now think about the house itself:

1 What building materials would be used for the walls and roof?

2 What would the floor be like?

3 Draw a picture to show what the one room inside the house would be like. There is one door and window. Decide what furniture there is. There were no cupboards then. People kept the few clothes they owned in a chest. Everything was made by the people who lived there, or the local carpenter. All food stores and animals were kept indoors in winter.

4 What do you think the old woman outside the house is doing?

5 Make a list of the disadvantages of living in this house.

This house is part of a sixteenth-century picture painted by Peter Bruegel in the Netherlands. Most ordinary people all over Europe lived in one-roomed houses like this, built with materials which were easy to get – often wattle and daub (branches woven together and plastered with dried mud and cow-dung).

Work in the country

A

B

C

The three pictures **A**, **B** and **C** show some of the main jobs which ordinary country people had to do through the year to grow the corn they needed for bread. The pictures have different dates. **A** comes from the margin of a book of psalms made about 1340, more than a hundred years before the Early Modern Age. **B** comes from a book of farming advice dated 1523. **C** was drawn about a hundred years later in the seventeenth century. These three pictures show that work and equipment in the country changed very little over the centuries. But one change did affect the countryside. England had only one important industry during most of the Early Modern Age – the wool and cloth trade. So big landowners made a lot of money from sheep-farming. Many of them changed from growing corn, and fenced in their fields for sheep.

1 About how many years are there between **A** and **C**?

2 **A**, **B** and **C** all show people ploughing. What is the main difference between the plough in **A**, and the ones in **B** and **C**? How much do you think the change helped? What animals are being used to pull the plough in each picture? (You can *just* see in **C**.)

3 Write down all the jobs being done in **C**, and make labelled sketches of each. Find the job mentioned on page 8, and add that.

4 Look at the picture of the shepherd. Obviously, when a landowner changed to sheep-farming, some of the people he had employed to grow corn would be out of a job. Discuss with the rest of the class the effect this might have on a small village (use pages 5–6).

At least six people were needed for every plough, to do all the jobs needed to grow and harvest corn throughout the year. How many people are looking after the sheep in this picture?

15

Food

Meals for ordinary people in the fifteenth and sixteenth centuries:

Almost all the time Food they produced or found themselves.	Coarse grey bread made from rye or barley. Only the rich ate fine white loaves made with wheat. Pot-herbs: beans, peas, onions, garlic, herbs, nettles and other plants in the hedgerows and woods. People usually made a kind of soup from any pot-herbs they had, and floated bread in it.
Sometimes If they kept cows and chickens, or could afford to buy	'White meat' (this meant milk, butter, cheese and eggs)
Very occasionally Most animals had to be killed in the winter – there was not enough fodder.	Beef, pork, ham or bacon smoked over the fire or salted.
Drink	Thin ale which they brewed themselves. No one knew about tea or coffee.

You can see that everyone usually had to live on what they could produce themselves. Bread was the most important thing they ate. If the corn harvest (barley, rye or oats) failed, they were in trouble in the winter. They needed the grain to make flour – but they also had to keep some of it for seed, to sow for next year's crop. If there was only a little grain, and everyone was hungry, it was not surprising that people often used almost all of it for flour. But then they had very little seed for next summer's harvest. So one bad harvest often meant two difficult years. Historians think that in the Early Modern Age about one harvest in every four or five was a bad one.

1 Look at the evidence on what rich people ate on page 3. Their meat was usually roasted, and served with rich sauces. Their banquets often finished with sugary pastry sometimes made into fantastic birds or buildings.
What was unhealthy about their diet, according to modern ideas about low fat, less sugar and plenty of fibre?

2 Was the diet of ordinary people healthier? What was the main danger for them? What areas in the modern world still face the same problems in finding enough to live on, as ordinary people did in Early Modern Britain?

People in towns

Towns were exciting, lively, crowded places. There were fewer of them in the Early Modern Age, and they were much smaller. They were usually the centre of several trades. Most towns still had walls, and gates which were firmly shut at dusk. But, on the whole, life was becoming safer, and some people were beginning to build houses outside the walls, where there was more space and fresh air.

York

York was a rich and bustling city, and the capital of the north of England. It had four miles of walls and was on the River Ouse. Merchants sent woollen cloth and other goods by river to Hull, from where they were shipped across to Europe. Goods went to the south of England by road or sea. These are some laws made by the City Council:

1517   No manner of person . . . shall cast any manner of filth . . . of *gougs* or dogs against Greyfriars Wall. [a goug may mean pig. Animals often wandered freely in towns.]

1520   No man . . . dwelling within this City . . . shall *suffer* [allow] their children to go with *clappers* [noisy rattles used to summon people to church] upon Shrove Tuesday and Good Friday . . . only the parish clerk shall go with the said clappers.

1524   No man dwelling on the waterbank of the Ouse shall cast any manner of filth or dung into the said water of the Ouse.

1526   Three *cornchapmen* [corn salesmen] to see to the Town Walls, to be kept clean . . . and to repair . . . the said walls now fallen.

1527   Every *Alderman* [member of the City Council] . . . shall hang a lantern with a light therein burning over their . . . door every night from five of the clock till nine of the clock on *pain of* a fine ['On pain of . . .' means 'the punishment for disobeying this rule will be . . .]

1530   All *strange* [from outside York] beggars now being within this City to the common nuisance shall *avoid* [leave] this City within 24 hours . . . on pain of *scourging* [whipping] of their bodies.

1 From the laws made in York, and the picture of the Shambles, make a list of problems likely to arise in towns. What do you think was the most serious problem?

2 Write down the list of trades in York, with meanings where necessary. Some are given. Use a dictionary if you need it. Label them using F for food, C for clothing, H for housing and L for luxury goods. Some trades may need L and another letter. What kind of goods produced in York do you think the merchants probably bought and sold?

3 What modern surnames can you find on the list?

A modern photograph of the Shambles, an old street in York, which has changed very little since the fifteenth century – and earlier. Think of the lack of fresh air and light for people who lived in these houses – and the fact that there were no modern taps or toilets indoors.

Trades in York	
Merchants	118
Fishers	47
Tanners	41
Tapiters	37
Tailors	87
Butchers	43
Weavers	39
Millers	35
Cordwainers	61
Bakers	41
Haberdashers	37
Carpenters	32
Cordwainers: Makers of luxury leather goods	
Tapiters: Makers of tapestries and other wall hangings	

How plague spread

Plague was a disease of black rats.

The black rat flourished in dirty conditions, especially in towns. It was bolder than the brown rat, and did not mind living near humans.

The rat flea lived on the black rat. When it fed on the rat's blood, the flea was infected with the plague bacteria.

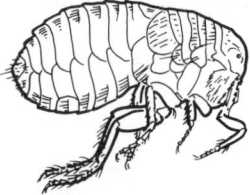

The rat died of plague. The flea got hungry – and looked around for another meal.

The flea survived for at least six weeks

in warm summer weather,

in plaster and thatch (many houses were built of these materials),

in bales of cloth, and in sacks of grain, flour and other food.

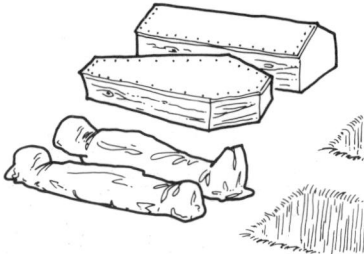

The flea usually went to live on nearby humans. They caught the plague from its bite – which introduced plague bacteria into the bloodstream.

Disease and medicine

There were many more dangerous diseases in the Early Modern Age. Diet must have had something to do with it. Ordinary people must have caught diseases much more easily when food was short, and their resistance was low. Rich people did not have that problem, but their health must have often suffered from too much of the wrong kind of food.

You have probably also realised that people lived in much dirtier conditions than now. As they did not have clean running water, from convenient taps indoors, they did not wash themselves or their clothes very often. In 1518 Erasmus, a Dutch scholar, visited several well-off English friends. This is what he said about their houses:

> The floors are generally . . . covered with rushes that are now and then removed, but not so as to disturb the foundation, which sometimes remains for about 20 years, nursing a collection of spittle, vomits, excrements of dogs and humans, spilt beer, and other filth I need not mention.

(It is quite difficult to think what Erasmus has not mentioned!)

One of the most serious diseases in the Early Modern Age was bubonic plague. Glands in the neck, under the arm and in the groin swelled into black painful abscesses; the patient became terribly ill, and usually died in a few days. Plague came in terrifying epidemics when thousands died. People knew it was very catching, but they did not know how it spread. Modern science has discovered this. As you can see in the diagram, rats and fleas both helped to cause plague – and there were plenty of both in towns of the Early Modern Age.

Remedies to stop the plague

A popular medicine (thought to be a remedy used by King Edward IV) was a sweet potion (mixture) of herbs – marigolds, rue and sorrel. It was said that if people drank it regularly, it would prevent the dreaded black swellings.

Bunches of rosemary – people sniffed these to stop plague spreading 'through the air'. In a London epidemic, their price went up from 12 to 60 pennies – the daily wage of a labourer was about 5 pennies.

Regulations made during a London epidemic in 1563, when about a quarter of the city's population died:

> Householders must light bonfires at the end of their street 'to consume the corrupt airs'. Windows in rooms where there were plague patients were opened so that their room could fill with smoke.

Searchers (usually old women) with white sticks went to check on houses where there were reports of illness. If they found the plague, the house was shut up for 40 days, and a white cross was painted on the door. No one could go in or out.

Each night carts collected the corpses of those who had died. They were buried in pits outside the city, 6 feet deep so dogs could not dig them up.

In this epidemic, Queen Elizabeth I went to Windsor. There were regulations there too:

> A gallows was put up. Anyone coming from London was to be hanged. Any Windsor citizen who had received goods from London had to leave their house – and the town.

1 Make an illustrated list of the real causes of bubonic plague. Think about living conditions, especially in towns, and how the plague might have spread, by trade for example. ◁3🗲 ◁4🗲

2 Explain:
   a) why plague epidemics usually started in the summer.
   b) why they usually started in towns, but could spread to the country. ◁4🗲

3 Make two columns headed 'Remedies which did no good' and 'Remedies which might have helped'. Fill in the columns giving your reasons. You may want to divide up the London regulations. ◁3🗲

4 You live in Windsor in 1563. You have a shop in the town, where you sell woollen cloth. Your family works for you. The Queen has just arrived at Windsor Castle, and you have just heard about the regulations she has made about the plague. You received two bales of expensive cloth from London yesterday, which you know you can sell. A carter (he is a friend of yours) is bringing some more cloth from London tomorrow.
   In a group, turn yourselves into this Windsor family and their neighbours and customers, and work out what you will do. ◁2🗲

Doctors and cures

In the Early Modern Age, doctors did not know about bacteria, or viruses, or how the human body works. It was difficult to find out too. For centuries, people had believed it was wrong to dissect (cut up) human or animal bodies. Even Arab doctors, who were usually more skilled than those in Europe, believed this.

Doctors in Europe based their ideas on the beliefs of the ancient Greeks. They thought the human body was made up of four 'humours' which were linked to the liquids in the body. These humours were: **sanguine, choleric, melancholy, phlegmatic**.

Look these words up in the dictionary. Three of them are old-fashioned (which ones?) but you will see that all four mean different kinds of moods. Copy the diagram in the margin, and by each humour draw a face to represent its mood. As you do this try to understand why people without modern medical knowledge might believe these ideas.

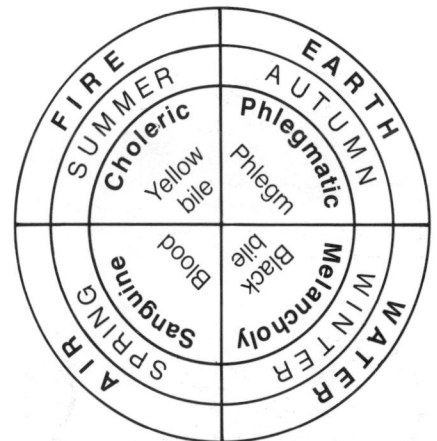

People believed that each humour was linked to the four things which made the world around them – earth, air, fire and water – and to one of the seasons too. So, for instance, a sanguine person was more likely to be cured in the spring.

CURES

Bleeding the patient to cure choleric or sanguine patients. Also used for fevers (even those caused by infected wounds where blood had been lost already). Doctors used leeches (blood-sucking worms) or 'cupped' a patient, drawing off blood.

Purges Medicines made from herbs which caused diarrhoea and vomiting, to cure patients with all kinds of ills, but especially phlegmatic or melancholy people.

Astrology Doctors believed that the stars helped them to cure their patients. They used the signs of the zodiac to decide the best time to give medicine, and when and where to bleed a patient.

DOCTORS

If you were very rich you could employ a **physician** when you were ill. He would have been trained in Latin, Greek, philosophy and astronomy. (Look up these words in the dictionary.)

He charged high fees, and his medicines were expensive too. He could use materials like powdered gold, amber and a unicorn's horn! (Where do you suppose he found that?)

Surgery was a terrible experience before there were any anaesthetics, but operations did take place. The picture shows 'trepanning' – drilling a hole in the skull, to cure headaches or mental illness.

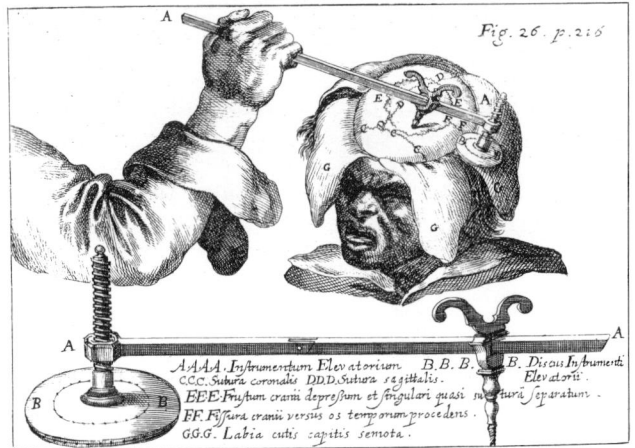

A **surgeon** was much less important than a physician. He was often a barber as well, paid like a carpenter or blacksmith, and used much the same tools. He was often a soldier like the one in this picture. He is removing an arrow from a very calm patient. Why will he almost certainly soon have more work?

Apothecaries sold purges and medicines, as well as herbs and spices. They had their own shops.

1 Make a list of the different jobs done by doctors and other medical staff in hospitals, health centres and chemist shops today. Which of them were closest to the three kinds of doctors on this page and page 20?

2 Which of the three kinds of doctors do you think was most likely to cure some of their patients?

3 Why are surgeons certainly not the lowest rank of doctors today?

Key words in this section to help you remember and understand what you have learnt. You should be able to use these words now and find evidence in the chapter which illustrates each of them.

Social classes
Nobles
Gentlemen
Merchants
Yeoman
Labourers

Women
Marriage
Dowry
Spinster
Widow

Children
Swaddling clothes
Manners
Punishments
Grammar schools
Lessons

Country people
Curfew
Rushlight
Wattle and daub
Ploughing
Sowing
Harvest

Food
Pot-herbs
White meat
Bread
Banquets

Towns
Walls
Gates
Beggars
Merchants
Tradesmen

Disease
Bubonic plague
Remedies
Bleeding
Purges
Physicians
Surgeons
Apothecaries

2 A changing world

How do you feel about using a computer? If you enjoy it, you can probably do a lot of different things with it. Computers are a new, modern and exciting tool for learning *and* enjoyment. No one had a computer in the Early Modern Age, of course. But many educated people then felt the same way about the ancient Greek language. It opened up a whole new world to them, just as computers do for us.

In the Middle Ages in Europe, churchmen were often the only people who could read and write – and teach. The Church taught that all learning and knowledge came from the Bible. But scholars (most of them still churchmen of course) also got more and more interested in the ancient Greeks, and in the Romans who followed them. These old civilisations seemed to hold the key to new and exciting discoveries about the world.

It seemed like a second beginning – a rebirth – in learning, art, new inventions and explorations. This chapter is about some of these changes in the Early Modern World. The label we usually use for them is the French word for rebirth – **The Renaissance**.

Artists explore space

Below is a picture on a wall in Chichester of the Virgin Mary and Jesus, painted long before the Renaissance, in the thirteenth century. The child cuddles up to his mother, and she leans tenderly over him. Artists have painted this special mother and child many times through the centuries. This artist (we do not know his name) obviously feels deeply about them. His picture is beautiful, but flat. The figures are not solid, and there is no space behind them. You may have learnt about **perspective** in art lessons, and how to make space, depth and distance in pictures. When this medieval artist worked, people did not think about that.

Discuss the problem of perspective with a partner, but each do your own drawings:

1 Trace the outline of the two figures. Then decide what you need to do to their clothes to make them seem more solid. Use colour and shading, and remember artists always gave Mary a blue robe. (Blue was their most expensive paint, made from the beautiful blue stone lapis lazuli.)

2 Now trace the shape behind the figures. It is the Virgin's throne. But is she sitting or standing? Why is it so difficult to decide? Try re-drawing the throne so that it looks as if you could really sit on it. (Work in rough first.) Can you make the two small angels in the background look further away? You will not make a better picture – just a different one.

Renaissance artists gradually discovered how to make space in their pictures, so that you feel you can walk far into the background. They found out how to use light and shade, as well as perspective, to make people and objects look solid.

Leonardo da Vinci

Leonardo da Vinci (1452–1519) was one of the most famous Renaissance artists. He came from a small village near Florence in Italy. He too painted the Virgin Mary and Jesus. Your experiments with the old wall painting should help you to see how much artists had discovered by the time Leonardo painted this *Virgin of the Rocks* in about 1506. Remember that a small black and white print in a book gives you only a little idea of this great picture, which is in the National Gallery, London. This is one of the few paintings Leonardo completed. He found it very difficult to finish a picture. He was never satisfied with what he had done.

Some other famous Renaissance artists
Giotto (*c.* 1267–1337)
Uccello (1397–1475)
Botticelli (1445–1510)
Raphael (1483–1520)
Michelangelo (1475–1564)

The extraordinary thing about Leonardo was that he could do so many other things as well as paint. He carved statues. He was an architect. He wrote poetry. He was a scientist, mathematician and inventor.

Leonardo's notebooks still exist. He filled them with everything he could discover or invent. (He wrote backwards from right to left – no one knows why, perhaps as a kind of code – and he could write equally well with both hands.) He cut up dead bodies, and sketched how the muscles and bones fitted together, so that he could paint people realistically. He was fascinated by flying and invented a flying machine, which might perhaps have flown if he had had a twentieth century engine to give it enough power.

Leonardo's Virgin wears a blue robe, which drapes round her outstretched arms as she reaches out to the young John the Baptist and her own baby. Jesus is a chubby baby, but there is something wise and special about him too. Leonardo uses light and shade to make his people realistic, and to take us far into a dark, mysterious rocky background.

■ Make lists in two columns to show the differences you can see between the pictures on these two pages. Think about the people, their faces, their clothes and the background. ◁✎

Part of a letter from Leonardo to the ruler of Milan

I have a sort of extremely light and strong bridge . . . to be most easily carried, and with it you may pursue, and at any time flee from the enemy . . . also methods of burning and destroying those of the enemy.

Again, I have kinds of *mortars* [heavy guns]; most convenient and easy to carry; and with these I can fling small stones almost resembling a storm; and with the smoke of these cause great terror to the enemy . . .

I will make covered chariots, safe and difficult to attack, which entering among the enemy . . . would break a body of men, however many there were. . . .

I would contrive catapults, *mangonels* [stone throwers] . . . and other machines . . . not in common use.

In time of peace I believe I can give perfect satisfaction . . . in the making of buildings public and private.

I can carry out sculpture in marble, bronze or clay, and also I can do in painting whatever may be done. . . .

And if any of the above named things seem impossible. . . . I am most ready to make the experiment in your park or in whatever place may please your Excellency.

1 Why has Leonardo written this letter?

2 What can you find out about the ruler of Milan from the letter?

3 Explain how drawing **B** worked in battle. Does Leonardo describe it in his letter? Choose another of Leonardo's suggestions and make a clear labelled drawing to show how it would work.

4 Write your own description of Leonardo da Vinci. Try to find out more about him if you can.

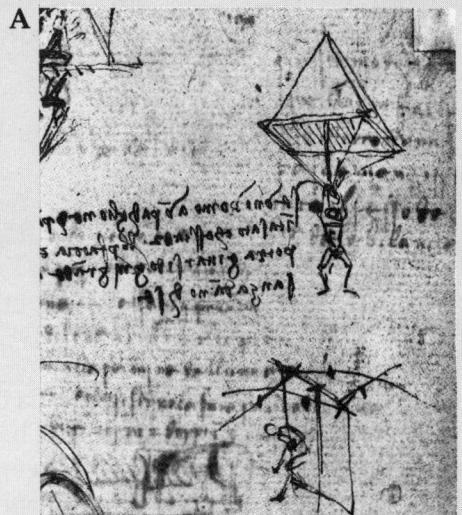

A

B

C

Printing: An invention which changed the world

This monk is writing an 'illuminated' manuscript (a book written by hand and decorated in colour) in about 1150. To do this he needs:

- the quill pen he holds, with the knife to sharpen it
- ink and expensive paints which he and his fellow monks make
- thin layers of real gold for extra decoration
- vellum to write on (this was sheepskin, stretched, smoothed, and polished – about 100 sheep were usually needed to provide enough pages of vellum for a book)
- a pumice stone to smooth the skin
- a goat or boar's tooth to polish it, and to use to rub out mistakes
- a great deal of time (we do not know how long)

The illuminated manuscript the monk finally produces will be very expensive. It will probably be kept chained up in a special library, or a church. To make another copy, he will have to start writing and decorating all over again.

The invention of printing came to Europe in the middle of the fifteenth century. This picture shows an early printing press. Find:

- workers preparing the type; they are working from written sheets
- a man putting ink on the type with a pad, so it is ready to go in the press
- a man removing a newly printed page
- blank paper waiting to be printed
- printed sheets waiting to be made into books.

The printed books these workers produce will not be as beautiful as the monk's illuminated manuscript. But they will be cheaper, and there will be many more of them.

Facts about printing

- Seven centuries before the Early Modern Age, the Chinese invented printing, using blocks of wood or stone, rather like potato printing which you may have done in art lessons.
- The first printing press in Europe was probably the one set up in Mainz, Germany, by a goldsmith called Gutenberg, in about 1450.
- William Caxton, a merchant, set up the first English printing press in Westminster in 1476.
- Andrew Miller (his name tells us his trade) set up the first Scottish printing press in Edinburgh in 1508.
- About this time, Europeans copied another Chinese invention: a method of making paper cheaply from rags and vegetable fibre.
- By 1500, there were about 20 million printed books in Europe. By 1600, it was about 200 million.

1 Why do you think the early printers were quite rich men?

2 What other invention besides printing helped them to do well?

3 How many times, and for what reasons have you read the printed word today? Think about food packets, notices, advertisements, etc. as well as books. Write down some differences in your life, if you lived in a world without printing.

4 Write down as many reasons as you can which explain why the invention of printing was so important.

Merchants had their own trade mark, used on all their goods. This is Caxton's, made from his initials.

Europe discovers the world

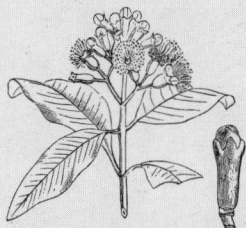

A fifteenth-century luxury: cloves. Pepper, mace and cinnamon were other expensive spices too. People dried or salted meat to preserve it, which made it tough and tasteless. So it is not surprising that they liked spicy sauces with it. But what kind of people could afford meat regularly anyway?

Luxuries from the East

Cloves and other spices came from the East. They were an expensive luxury in fifteenth-century Europe. Other luxuries from the East were rare and expensive too – jewels, fine silks and cottons, and dyes made from tropical woods and even beetles (cochineal).

Arab traders brought these goods from the East by a long and difficult overland route to the shores of the Eastern Mediterranean. There, Italian merchants from the rich trading cities of Venice and Genoa bought them to sell at a big profit in Europe.

1 Make an illustrated list of luxuries from the East. Write down reasons why they were scarce and expensive.

2 Find out in a supermarket how much cloves and pepper cost now. Are they still a luxury? If not, why not?

> Use the map on page 29 as you read these pages.

The East seemed an unknown and wonderful place to Europeans – where people might make their fortunes and perhaps even find a mountain of gold. So European explorers wanted to find a new way to the East by sea. Somewhere beyond the huge unknown Atlantic Ocean was the goal: 'The Indies' (India and the 'Spice Islands') and Cathay (China). But where?

Christopher Columbus, a sailor from Genoa, was quite sure *he* knew. Since the world was round (and most educated people believed that by now) Christopher Columbus was certain he must sail *west* to reach the riches of the East. He worked out the distance too. He thought Cathay was about 4000 miles away. But for a long time, no one took him seriously.

Finally he persuaded the King and Queen of Spain to give him three small ships – the *Pinta*, the *Niña*, and the *Santa Maria*. Their crews were mostly unemployed ex-prisoners.

In 1492 he set out from Spain. He was lucky, for the weather stayed good. But as the ships sailed further and further away from home, the sailors began to grumble. So Columbus kept two log books. One showed the real distance they had sailed. The other, which the crew saw, recorded a much shorter distance from home. After 33 days they saw land birds and floating weed. Finally they saw land.

Columbus had reached the Caribbean. Later he landed on the shores of South America. He never realised he had found a new continent. He was always certain he had reached 'The Indies'. So the islands he explored became 'The West Indies'. He called the people he found living there 'Indians'. (Europeans went on using that name for the people they found in North and South America, even when they knew they were not from the Indies.)

Another explorer, Amerigo Vespucci, realised there was a huge unknown continent. A German mapmaker named the new continent after Amerigo – America.

We do not know exactly what Columbus's ship, the Santa Maria *looked like. However, this picture dated 1483 gives us a good idea. The* Santa Maria *was about 29 metres long. Pace this distance out in the corridor or playground. Forty people lived in that space.*

Columbus's four voyages led to a Spanish Empire (new lands ruled by Spain) in this 'New World'.

Sailing round Africa

Meanwhile Portuguese sailors were finding another route to the East, round the huge continent of Africa. In 1497 **Vasco da Gama** finally sailed into the Indian Ocean. Arab sailors showed him the way to India. Once there, he loaded his ships with spices. The Portuguese too began to make an empire.

Round the world

In 1519 **Ferdinand Magellan** sailed with five ships from Spain. He was determined to find a way right round the world. His sailors were not so sure. By the time he reached the southern tip of South America he had already crushed a serious mutiny. One ship turned back home, as the expedition sailed into the stormy strip of sea full of treacherous rocks now called the Strait of Magellan. After 38 terrifying days they found their way into a vast peaceful ocean which no European had ever sailed before. They were so relieved they called it the Pacific Ocean. But it was far bigger than they realised, and stores were running out.

It took 96 days to reach the Spice Islands. The sailors who were still alive were sick and starving. Their luck did not improve. When they landed, Magellan was killed in a fight with hostile islanders. Only one ship, the *Victoria*, got back to Spain in 1522. She had 2½ tonnes of cloves on board – and 18 sick, hungry sailors (280 had set out in 1519). But she had sailed right round the world.

Columbus, da Gama and Magellan are just three of many European explorers who discovered the rest of the world. They came from Spain and Portugal. Soon English, French and Dutch explorers joined in. Trade grew; European people began to settle in new lands and sometimes fought each other for them. New goods came into Europe: potatoes, tomatoes, tobacco, and later cocoa, tea and coffee. Sugar became more and more plentiful.

It is easy to forget the people who already lived in the lands Europeans found. The civilised and skilled peoples of the East never wanted to explore Europe. They did not think much of Europeans – they found them dirty and uncivilised. For many people in the New World, Europeans brought only trouble. The 'Indians' in the Caribbean and South America suffered terribly in European wars and from European diseases.

The great European discoveries linked the world together in a new way. But an old problem grew bigger: How do people of different races and cultures learn to live together, and to respect each other?

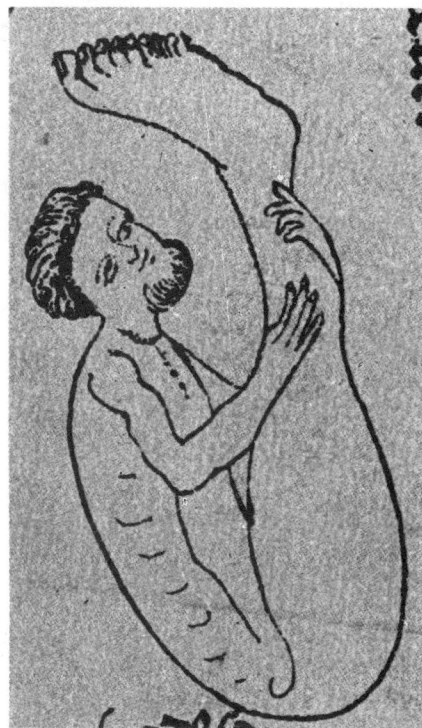

Fears of the unknown: explorers feared they might meet all kinds of strange monsters on land and sea. This picture of a one-legged man shading himself with his huge foot comes from a fourteenth-century French manuscript. The seas might hold terrors too.

■ You are a fifteenth-century explorer. You catch a glimpse of a whale at sea, and a rhinoceros on land. Illustrate and describe your 'monsters' to show people when you get home.

1 Use a world map in a modern atlas to work out how far Columbus was wrong in his calculation of the distance between Spain and China. Measure a direct route with a ruler.

2 Find a map of ocean currents in a modern atlas. How do they help to tell us why Columbus reached the Caribbean quite quickly?

3 In class discussion, think of words to describe Columbus and Magellan. Make a list of results of their discoveries. Try to sort out the good results from the bad.

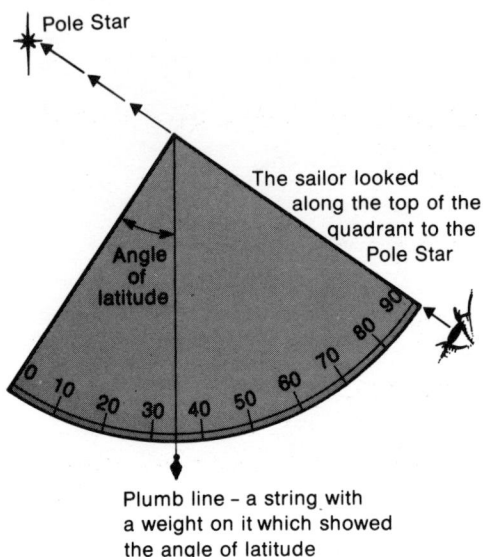

Pole Star

The sailor looked along the top of the quadrant to the Pole Star

Angle of latitude

Plumb line – a string with a weight on it which showed the angle of latitude

A quadrant. Sailors used this instrument to work out their angle of latitude, which helped to tell them how far they had sailed from Home. You could try making your own quadrant with card, string and Plasticine as a weight for the plumb line. Use a protractor to mark the angles accurately.

A sixteenth-century ship's compass.

On board ship

Life on board ship was tough and dangerous. Ships were dirty and very cramped. There were rats, fleas, lice and beetles below decks. Any disease spread quickly. The captain had a cabin, but sailors had little shelter and usually slept on deck except in really bad storms. There were no modern waterproof materials to keep them dry.

Food and drink were stored in wooden barrels. Hard tasteless ship's biscuits were the main food. But even these soon got weevils in them, and on a long voyage could become a slimy mess. Sailors took anything that would keep – peas, beans, onions, garlic, cheese and salted meat. But nothing kept for a long time. When the weather was calm enough, they cooked hot food on a fire in a box of sand. Wine, beer and water soon went bad too. One of the worst problems on long voyages was **scurvy**, a dangerous and painful disease caused by lack of fresh fruit and vegetables.

The work was hard too. It was a dangerous climb up the rigging to adjust the sails high above the swaying deck, even when the weather was quite calm. In rough weather it was far worse. Captains were always worried their crews might make trouble, so they kept them busy. Day and night were divided into four-hour 'watches', and the crew took turns to be on watch. Twice a day, the captain held a religious service. In calm weather, the men might fish or sing to while away the time. In rough weather, everyone had plenty to do. Punishments were harsh. A sailor who disobeyed orders was whipped or put in iron chains. Death was the punishment for mutiny.

Finding the way was difficult. Maps either did not exist, or were very inaccurate. A compass was still a sailor's most useful instrument. Quadrants helped to work out latitude. But the stories of the three explorers you have just read show how difficult it was for sailors out of sight of land to know where they were.

1 Write down the materials used to build a sixteenth-century sailing ship. Why was a cooking fire kept in a box of sand? ← 26 ◁1◁

2 Make a list of the dangers on board ship. Look up scurvy in the dictionary. What other diseases might sailors get? ← 18 ◁1◁

3 Read page 29 and then write a sentence about each of the following problems for explorers:
 a) finding a rich person to back you
 b) finding the way
 c) stores for the journey
 d) the crew. ◁3◁

4 Why do you think sailors went on journeys of exploration, in spite of all the hardship? ◁2◁

5 Make your own compass. You need: card, a small shallow dish (a cut-down plastic carton will do), a needle, a drinking straw, a magnet.

1 Cut out a circle of card a bit bigger than your dish.
2 Divide circle into four equal sections and mark each of the four points of the compass – north, south, east and west.
3 Fill the dish with water and put it on your circle of card.
4 Magnetise the needle by stroking it with the magnet.
5 Place the needle inside a small piece of the straw.
6 Float the straw on the water and the magnetised needle will swing round to point to the north.
7 Adjust your circle of card to line up north with the needle.

Why would your compass not be much good on board ship? How is a ship's compass designed? ◁4◁

Evidence about Magellan's journey

Some of the supplies Magellan took with him:

9700 kg biscuits
258 kg salt beef
238 dozen dried fish
200 barrels of sardines
508 kg cheese
Sacks of peas, beans, lentils, flour, honey, onions, figs and salt
2310 kg gunpowder
82 heavy guns on trolleys
Smaller guns, armour, pikes, and crossbows
Brass bracelets. Lengths of velvet. 500 looking glasses.

One of Magellan's crew kept a diary. He said he went on the voyage

> to experiment and see with my eyes a part of the very great and awful things of the Ocean.

This is how he describes what it was like towards the end of 96 days in the Pacific:

> We ate old biscuit reduced to powder and full of grubs, and drank water that was yellow and stinking . . . we ate *oxhide* [leather] . . ., also the sawdust of wood, and rats, which cost *half a crown each* [this was a large sum]. . . . the worst misfortune was that the gums of our men grew so much that they could not eat, and nineteen died.

1 Describe a meal that an ordinary sailor might eat
a) soon after setting sail
b) after the ship had been away from home for six months.
(He might be lucky and catch some fresh fish.)

2 How can you tell that Magellan's sailors are likely to get scurvy?

3 Was Magellan expecting trouble? Explain your answer.

4 How would Magellan expect to use the last three items?

1 What disease have many of the sailors on Magellan's ship obviously got?

2 Copy out the following filling in the blanks:

Ferdinand Magellan wanted to sail round the world. The Emperor Charles V, ruler of Spain gave him _____ ships. They were so old it took Magellan a year to repair them. In _____ Magellan set sail.

Now finish the story of Magellan's journey, using the information on these pages, and pages 26–7.

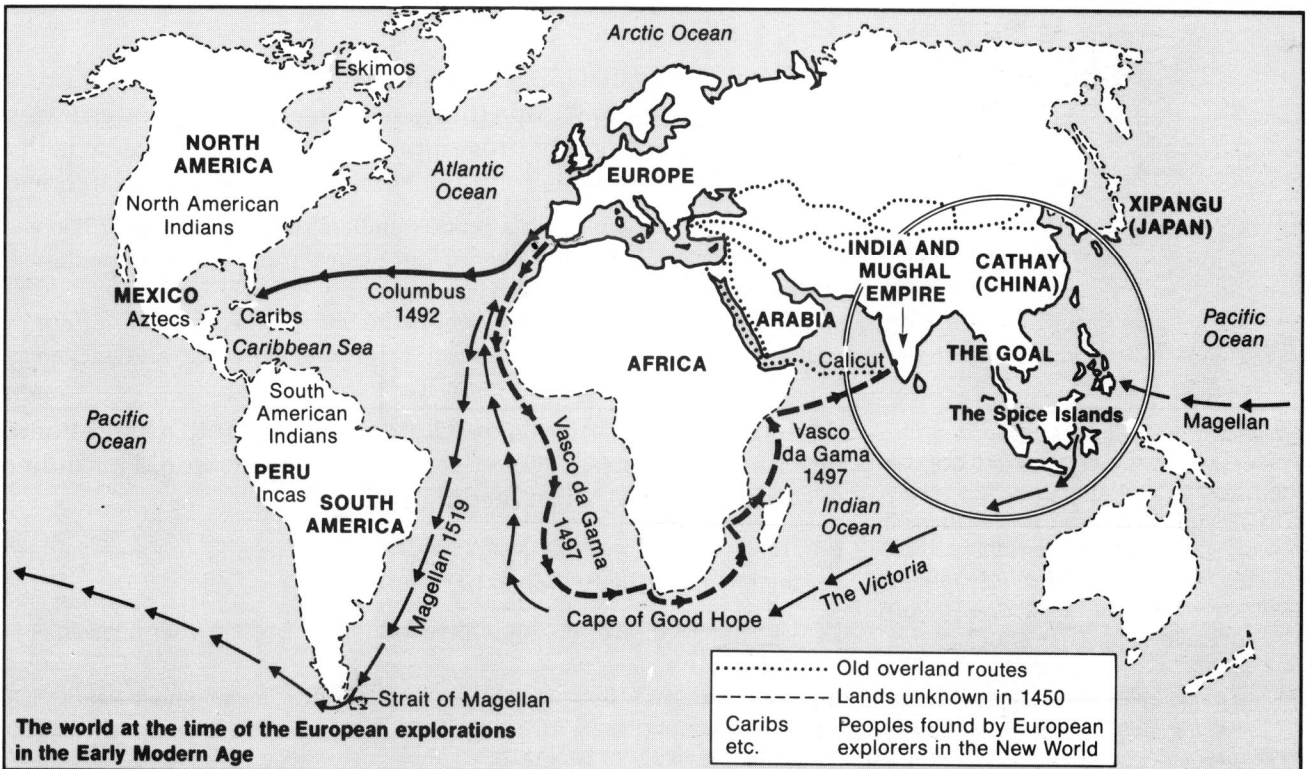

The world at the time of the European explorations in the Early Modern Age

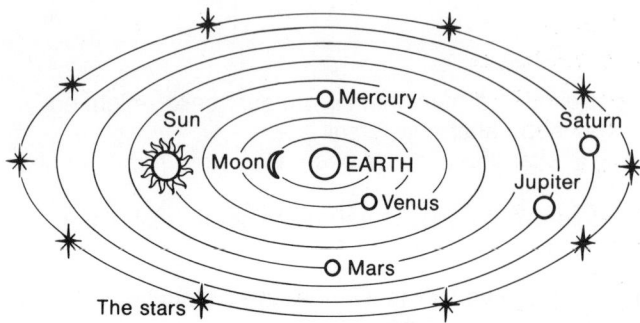

Diagram labels: Sun, Moon, EARTH, Mercury, Venus, Mars, Jupiter, Saturn, The stars

The sun and the earth

This diagram shows what Aristotle, an ancient Greek thinker, thought the universe was like. The earth was the fixed centre, and the sun, the planets and the stars on the outer edge all revolved round it. Huge glassy walls kept everything in place. People believed this for centuries. The Catholic Church took over the idea. God had created the earth, so of course it was the centre of the universe.

Renaissance scholars began to work out that the earth went round the sun, but they could not prove it. And it was dangerous to question the beliefs of the Church. **Copernicus** (1473–1543) only published his book explaining this new idea when he was an old man, near to death. **Giordano Bruno** (1548–1600) was burnt at the stake because he said there might be other suns and planets in the universe too.

Galileo (1564–1642)

Galileo came from Pisa, Italy. He was a short, red-headed man with lots of energy. He was a brilliant mathematician, and loved inventing things. He made many kinds of instruments for measuring and calculating. He used experiments to prove his ideas. We take this for granted now, but it was a completely new way for a scientist to work then. He is said to have gone to the top of the leaning tower in Pisa, and dropped two objects of different weights. They both reached the ground at the same time. Until then, people thought that heavy objects dropped faster than light ones. Galileo proved them wrong.

Galileo was sure that Copernicus was right. In 1609 he became the first man to use a telescope to observe the stars in a modern way. His observations finally proved the centre of our universe is the sun, and the earth goes round it. He wrote about his discoveries:

> I have seen stars in *myriads* [huge numbers] which have never been seen before . . . I have discovered four planets [round Jupiter], neither known nor observed by anyone before my time . . .
> It is a most beautiful sight to behold the body of the moon . . . it does not possess a smooth and polished surface, but one rough and uneven . . . just like the face of the earth itself.

An English visitor to Italy, Sir Henry Wotton, wrote a letter home describing Galileo's discoveries. He said Galileo would be 'either exceeding famous, or exceeding ridiculous.'

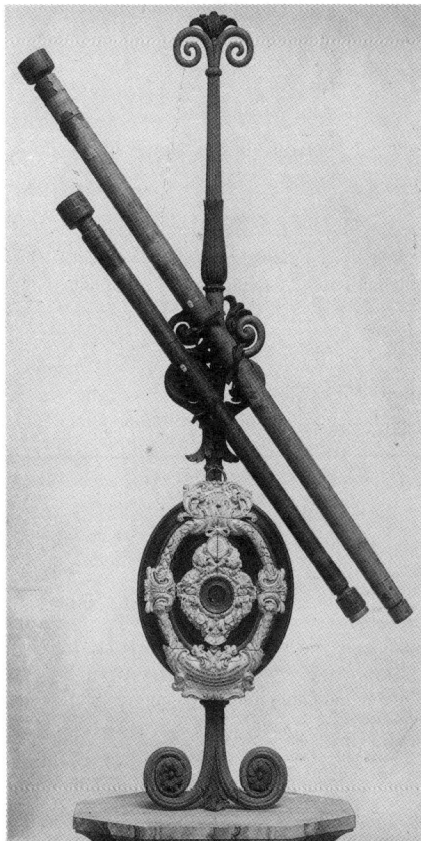

Galileo's telescope – probably the first one he made in 1609. He got the idea from a Dutch spectacle maker, who discovered that if he looked through two lenses together, they made distant objects much larger. Galileo made his telescope much stronger. He said, 'The effect of this instrument is to represent an object . . . 50 miles away, as large as if it was 5.' It was the first modern astronomer's instrument.

1 What are Galileo's two discoveries which he describes here? Do you think that Sir Henry Wotton believes in them?

2 Does Galileo have any doubts about them? Explain your answer.

3 We do not know for sure that the experiment on the leaning tower of Pisa actually happened. Why do you think a story like this got around? Do you think it is likely to be true?

Galileo was an old man and going blind when his book about his discoveries was finally published. The leaders of the Catholic Church accused him of wrong beliefs and put him on trial. His judges showed him horrible instruments of torture and threatened him with death. This is part of a statement he then signed:

> I, Galileo . . . aged seventy . . . kneeling before you, swear that I have always believed . . . all that is held, preached and taught by the Holy . . . Catholic Church. I must altogether abandon the false belief that the sun is the centre of the world and immovable, and the earth is not the centre of the world, and moves . . . I swear I will not say or write anything which makes people suspect that this is still my belief.

Galileo was kept a prisoner in his home until he died. But nothing could alter what he had discovered. His forbidden book proved as a scientific fact that the earth moved round the sun. The book is still famous today.

1 You are a friend of Galileo. Describe what happened at his trial. Bring in Galileo's appearance and character, your opinion of his discoveries, and how you feel about his punishment.

2 Copy the diagram showing Aristotle's idea of the universe. (You can use a compass and make full circles if you prefer.) Then make the same kind of diagram showing the solar system we know about today: the sun (in the centre), Mercury, Venus, Earth (and moon), Mars, Jupiter, Saturn, Uranus, Neptune, Pluto (usually the furthest out in space). If you can, find out from an encyclopedia when the extra planets were discovered. Mark the dates on your diagram.

Trouble in the church

This is St Peter's Church in Rome. It is one of the grandest churches in Europe, with a dome designed by the artist Michelangelo. The Pope who ordered the building of St Peter's in 1506 wanted to impress everyone with the power of the Church. He thought a huge and beautiful church helped people to worship God. But many people who were worried about the Church anyway thought St Peter's cost far too much, and that the Pope and other important churchmen were much too interested in wealth and power.

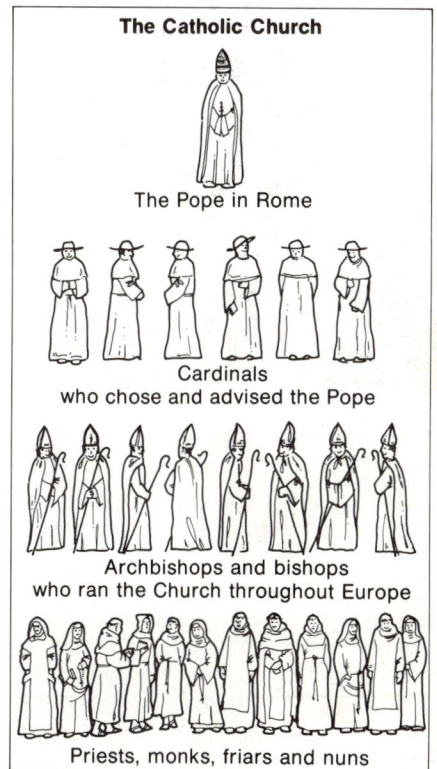

The Catholic Church

The Pope in Rome

Cardinals
who chose and advised the Pope

Archbishops and bishops
who ran the Church throughout Europe

Priests, monks, friars and nuns

Martin Luther (1483–1546)

Matin Luther was a German monk who was very worried about the Church. He was a serious, clever man who could be fiery and tough. He became a professor at the University of Wittenberg. The Pope wanted to raise more money to build St Peter's. So he said that people could buy pardons for their sins. These pardons were sold all over Germany. Luther believed they were wrong – people could not *buy* forgiveness for their sins. In 1517 he wrote out 95 reasons why he disagreed with the Pope, and nailed them on the church door at Wittenberg where everyone would see them. They were printed too, so people all over Germany could read them.

Luther went further. He said people must read the Bible themselves. This would give them real faith, so they could follow the teachings of Jesus in their lives. They did not need the Pope and priests and monks to help them. All Germany was buzzing with his arguments.

The Pope was determined to crush Luther, and sent him a special proclamation (called a 'Bull') which expelled him from the Church. Luther took this grand official document into the market place in Wittenberg, and publicly burnt it.

Luther might have been burnt himself for disobeying the Pope. But the ruler of Saxony where he lived protected him. He spent the rest of his life teaching and writing. He translated the Bible into German. He married a woman who had been a nun (the Church did not allow monks and nuns to marry) and had six children.

Protestants

People who agreed with Luther *protested* against the Pope and the Catholic Church. They soon got a nickname – **Protest-ants**. They believed that everyone must work out their own faith from the Bible, and they often disagreed with each other. So different Protestant churches grew up. But they all agreed on one thing. They were not part of the Catholic Church, and they condemned the Pope. There was no longer one Catholic Church in western Europe. The table opposite will help you to see the differences between Catholics and Protestants. We call this splitting up of the Christian Church **The Reformation**.

Sadly the split between Catholic and Protestant Christians led to hatred, war and persecution. Catholics and Protestants attacked each other in cartoons too. Here a Protestant artist shows the Pope being sent down to Hell by all kinds of terrible monsters. The two pictures of the Monk on the right go together. The monk looks quite reasonable in the first picture as he listens to a poor widow and her child. What do you think they want? But in the second picture you lift a flap to see what he is really like. What does the Protestant artist think of monks? Is it reliable evidence?

Catholics	Protestants
Loyal to the Pope in Rome.	Did not accept the Pope.
Bishops, priests, monks and nuns.	No monks and nuns.
When Luther broke away, the Catholic Church did a great deal to reform (change things for the better).	Some Protestant churches kept bishops. Others believed that people in local churches should choose their minister and run their own affairs.
Services in Latin. The priest took the most important part.	**Services** in people's own language. People joined in the service more. Reading the Bible was very important.
Churches were beautifully decorated with pictures and statues. Catholics thought this helped people to worship God.	**Churches** were plain with no pictures or statues. Protestants thought these made people superstitious.

Key words in this chapter to help you remember and understand what you have learnt. You should be able to use these words now and find evidence in the chapter which illustrates each of them.

Renaissance
civilisation
perspective
foreground
background
architect
painter

Printing
illuminated manuscript
vellum
paper
printing press

Explorations
luxuries
The Indies
log book
continent
mutiny
scurvy
compass
quadrant
race
culture
empire

The universe
astronomer
planets
stars
the solar system
telescope
scientific fact

Reformation
(The meanings are given of some important words you will meet later)
Catholic
Protestant
Superstitious
Bull
Pope
cardinal
bishop
monk
nun
excommunication: being expelled from the Church
heresy: beliefs which are different from the official teaching of the Church
heretic: someone who holds beliefs different from the Church's teaching
Inquisition: a special court of the Church used to condemn heresy
to recant: to go back on one's beliefs and admit they were false

3 Kings: Good, bad or a bit of both?

This is what people expected a successful ruler to be like:
- royal, grown-up and male,
- good looking, with a grand court
- religious and care for the Church
- brave and successful in war
- his queen must have royal blood, she must give him sons and not interfere with his job of running the country
- he must organise his money well and not ask for heavy taxes
- he must control the country, especially the nobles.

■ Discuss in class why people in the Early Modern Age thought these ideas were so important. ◁4▷

The unknown artist who painted this portrait of Henry VI probably never saw him. He does not make the king look very impressive – but that may be because he was not a very good artist. Henry did not care what he looked like. Once a crowd jeered because he was wearing an old blue gown, 'as if he had no more to change into'.

Henry VI (reigned 1422–61; 1470–1)

He was a king who had problems. Here are some facts about him:
- His family were the Lancastrians. He became King of England when he was a baby of nine months. He was crowned with a bracelet. The nobles who had to rule for him were very jealous of each other.
- When he was grown up, fighting began in England, because some nobles thought he should not be king. He was never in the thick of it. He was taken prisoner three times – because he did not even seem to realise when he ought to run away.
- He was very religious, and built two beautiful churches in Eton and Cambridge.
- He married a French princess, Margaret of Anjou. She was a strong character and interfered a lot. She became very unpopular. After eight years they had a son.
- Being a king seemed too much for Henry, and he became mentally ill. He would often sit staring into space, and refuse to decide anything.

Evidence about Henry VI

A A priest in his household wrote long after Henry was dead:

> This king was a serious and sincere worshipper of God. He was more suited to prayer than to dealing with worldly things

B An observer who supported Henry's enemies said in 1459:

> The king was simple and led by greedy advisers ... his debts increased daily ... and such taxes as were put on the people were spent in vain for he held no household (did not have a grand court) nor went to war ... the Queen and her supporters ruled the realm as they liked, gathering riches innumerable.

■ Draw a table like this and give Henry points out of 5 under each heading, e.g. 2 for Marriage, but no more because his wife interfered. ◁3▷

King	Appearance	Character	A grand court	Religion	Marriage	War	Money	Total
Henry VI								

Edward IV (reigned 1461–70; 1471–83)

In 1461 England had a new king. Edward IV belonged to another part of the royal family, the Yorkists. He was only 18, and he won his crown because he defeated Henry VI in battle. Edward IV too had his ups and downs:

- He married a rather poor but beautiful widow called Elizabeth Woodville. She was not royal, and she and her family did well out of her grand new position as queen. They were very unpopular. Edward and Elizabeth had two sons and four daughters.
- The Lancastrians defeated Edward in 1470–1. They put Henry VI back on the throne and Edward fled abroad. But he came back and defeated his enemies. On the night he returned to London as king, Henry VI was murdered in the Tower. Probably Edward ordered it.
- He managed his money well, although he spent a lot (see below). He kept accounts carefully, encouraged trade and looked after royal lands well. So he did not have to ask for many taxes.
- He built a beautiful church – St George's Chapel, Windsor. But people did not think he was religious like Henry VI.

Probably the artist who painted this portrait of Edward IV had only heard about the king, and not seen him. From the written accounts of Edward's appearance, he was probably a good deal better looking than this.

Evidence about Edward IV

A Edward's appearance.

Everyone agreed that Edward was very handsome when he was young. This is what a foreign visitor wrote:

> Edward was of a gentle nature and cheerful aspect: nevertheless should he assume an angry countenance he could appear very terrible to beholders ... in food and drink he was most immoderate; it was his habit so I have learned to take an *emetic* [a medicine which causes vomiting] for the delight of gorging his stomach once more. For this reason ... he had grown fat in the loins.

B Edward's skeleton.

This was measured over 300 years after he died, when his coffin was opened. He was 1.92 metres tall and broad too. The average height for an adult male then was about 25 cm shorter.

C Edward's clothes and jewels.

Edward's accounts show he spent about £2000 a year on clothes and furs. (It cost a noble about £1000 a year to run his household) These are some of the materials and jewels he bought in 1480:

> Black velvet lined with purple
> White damask lined with sable fur
> Purple cloth of gold, lined with ermine
> A flower of gold, with a pointed diamond, four rubies, four pearls
> Four rings of gold decorated with four rubies

1 You are a noble who thinks he ought to be king. Draw a picture of yourself. What should you put in to make you look like a king? Underneath write a reference for yourself, explaining why you would make a good king. Use the points in the box opposite. Begin:

> My trusty nobles: there are many reasons why I should be your king . . .

2 Add a score for Edward to your diagram. Take a survey through the class of the scores of both kings. What do you think of the result?

3 Trace the outline of Edward IV's portrait. Use some of the material he bought as a guide, and colour his clothes. He can wear the jewel – and one of the rings. Use a dictionary for difficult words.

4 You are a Yorkist noble. Write to a Lancastrian, explaining why you support Edward IV.

A fifteenth-century battle was often like the confusing scene in this picture. Heavy guns, or cannons, which used gunpowder, were a new, frightening weapon. They were noisy, and made battles smoky and even more confusing. They could destroy thick castle walls, and cause terrible death and suffering. But they were expensive, heavy and difficult to move. They often missed their target. There is no sign of one here. In battles like this, the real fighting was done on foot, and it was muddled, bloody and cruel.

1 Which weapon is causing the most damage to men and horses?

2 Why are the banners so important in a battle like this?

3 Look up siege in a dictionary. Why were cannons used mostly in sieges in the fifteenth century, and not in battles like this one?

Find in the picture:
*The **knights** in armour from head to toe; they are nobles. They were expected to be in the thick of the fight. Many of them had their own private armies. A **king** (look on the right). How has the artist shown that he is the most important person? He was expected to be in the fight too. The **archers**. They are using longbows (look up longbow in a dictionary). Are they as well protected as the knights? They are ordinary soldiers who could not afford full armour.*

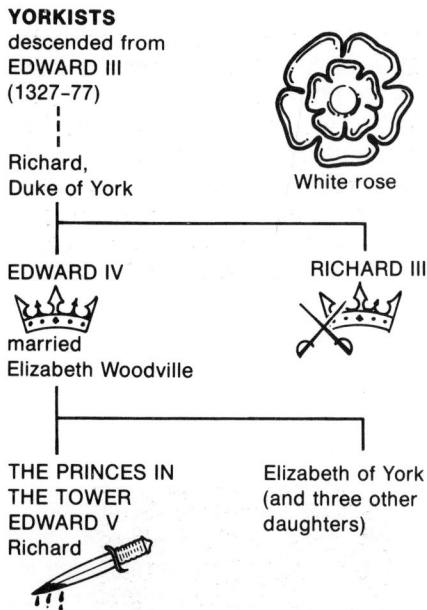

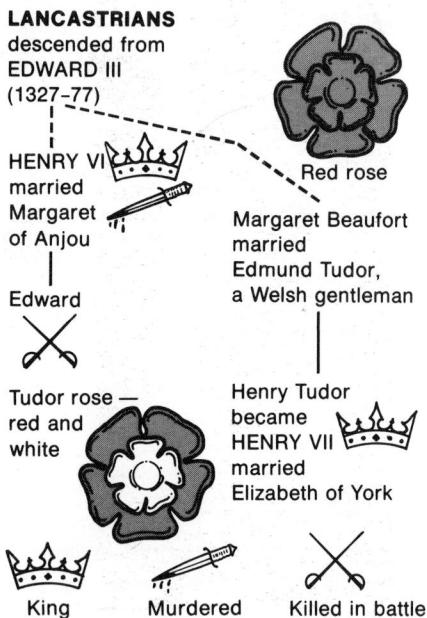

The Wars of the Roses

There were battles like this in England from 1460 to 1485, between the Lancastrians and the Yorkists, about who should be King. In the margin you can see how Henry VI, Edward IV and Henry Tudor fit into those families. The Lancastrians sometimes used a red rose as their badge, and the Yorkists a white one. So these wars are called the Wars of the Roses. They lasted 25 years, but the times when there was any actual fighting were much shorter – about 13 weeks. England was quite peaceful in between. The lives of ordinary people went on much as usual, unless they were unlucky enough to live where a battle was fought. Merchants carried on their trading. It was a power struggle amongst the top people about which king should rule and how.

■ What new invention that had nothing to do with war came into England during the Wars of the Roses? ← 24–5

YORKISTS
descended from
EDWARD III
(1327–77)

Richard,
Duke of York

White rose

EDWARD IV
married
Elizabeth Woodville

RICHARD III

THE PRINCES IN
THE TOWER
EDWARD V
Richard

Elizabeth of York
(and three other
daughters)

LANCASTRIANS
descended from
EDWARD III
(1327–77)

HENRY VI
married
Margaret
of Anjou

Red rose

Edward

Margaret Beaufort
married
Edmund Tudor,
a Welsh gentleman

Tudor rose —
red and
white

Henry Tudor
became
HENRY VII
married
Elizabeth of York

King   Murdered   Killed in battle

The Princes in the Tower

Edward IV was 40 when he died suddenly in April 1483. His sons were Edward, who was 12 and Richard (Duke of York), who was 10. The old problem was back again. Who would rule until the 12-year-old Edward V was old enough to take over? Before Edward IV died, he gave the job to his loyal younger brother, Richard of Gloucester.

This is what happened

April 1483 Edward V stayed in the Tower of London, to get ready for his coronation. This was what a new king normally did. His younger brother joined him.

June 1483 Richard of Gloucester suddenly announced that Edward IV and Elizabeth Woodville had not been legally married. So neither of the two 'Princes in the Tower' had a right to be king.

July 1483 Richard of Gloucester was crowned Richard III.

From August 1483 No one saw the two princes playing in the garden any more. Rumours began that they had been murdered. They were never seen again.

1483–5 Richard III became very unpopular. People thought he was the murderer. Otherwise he ruled well, but he had little time.

August 1485 Henry Tudor (the last Lancastrian, who had been in exile in France) landed in Wales and marched into England. At the battle of Bosworth, Richard III was killed. Henry Tudor became King Henry VII – the first Tudor monarch.

This portrait of Richard III was painted after his death, from a portrait by an artist who had seen Richard. So it is another portrait which only gives an impression of what he might have looked like. In Tudor times, people said Richard was a wicked murderer, and also a crippled hunchback. Why do you think they said that?

Were the princes murdered?

A murderer needs a *motive*. A murderer must have an *opportunity*.

Was Richard III the murderer?

Motive Did Richard need to murder the princes, as he had said they were not royal? Or were they still a threat to him as King? If he had not murdered them, why did he not produce them to stop the rumours?

Opportunity As King, Richard could get into the Tower any time.

Was Henry VII the murderer?

Motive The princes were much more royal than Henry, so they were a threat to him. Henry could not say they were not royal – he had married their sister.

Opportunity If the princes were still alive when Henry became king in 1485, he could easily have done it. But if they were alive, where had they been for two years?

■ Find out more if you can. Hold a class debate on whether Richard III was the murderer.

In 1674 workmen found some bones in the Tower of London. Did they belong to the prince? The bones were buried in Westminster Abbey. This photograph was taken in 1933 when scientists examined them. It shows the leg bones of two children aged about 12 and 10, but they could be girls or boys. No one has solved the mystery.

The first Tudor: Henry VII (1485–1509)

Henry VII won his crown because he won the battle of Bosworth, and Richard III was killed. Many nobles thought he would not last long. Other people might try to win the crown by rebelling.

But Henry behaved like a king straight away. Richard III's naked corpse was slung over a mule, and taken into nearby Leicester so that everyone could see it – very dead. Henry had a grand coronation. He soon married Edward IV's eldest daughter, Elizabeth of York. She was everything that a queen was expected to be (unlike the other two you have met). She bore Henry a son a year later – and several more children. She seems to have been a quiet, gentle girl and never interfered.

Rebellions Henry had some trouble. Perkin Warbeck was a 17-year-old boy, who worked for a silk merchant in the Netherlands. He pretended he was the younger of the two princes in the Tower. This was clever, since no one knew where the princes were. Perkin was a danger because Henry's enemies helped him. James IV, King of Scotland, used him to make trouble for Henry. He invaded the north of England in 1496. The next year Perkin landed in Cornwall, but he was soon captured, and in the end Henry executed him.

Nobles Henry knew he had to get on well with his nobles, and keep them in order too. He was not always tough on them. The powerful Earl of Surrey was a good soldier but he had fought against Henry at Bosworth. Henry put him in the Tower and took some of his lands. But the king needed good soldiers. Four years later he put the Earl in charge of the north of England. He served Henry loyally, especially when the Scots invaded.

Money Henry could be tough if he wanted. He used fines to punish nobles who disobeyed him. This was useful. It made him rich and made the disobedient nobles poor – and less likely to cause trouble. But it made him unpopular too.

Henry was as good at managing his money as Edward IV had been, and used the same methods. He left a lot of money when he died – enough to run the country for two years.

Marriages In the margin you can see the important marriages Henry arranged for three of his children. His reign lasted 25 years – he died when his son Henry VIII was just grown up. The Tudors were safe.

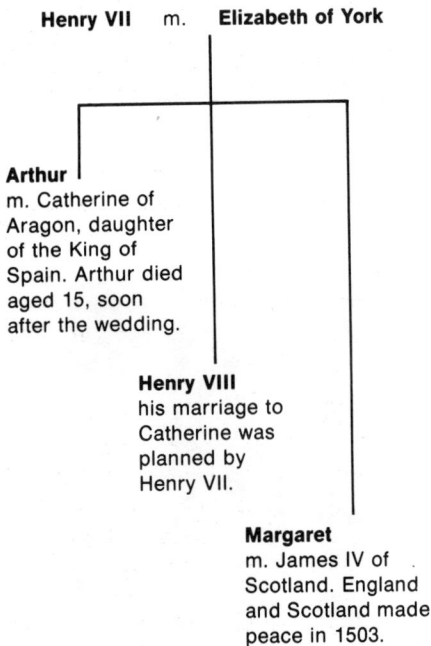

The Tudor rose – the badge of the Tudors. When Henry VII married Elizabeth of York, he combined the red rose of Lancaster with the white rose of York.

Henry VII m. **Elizabeth of York**

Arthur
m. Catherine of Aragon, daughter of the King of Spain. Arthur died aged 15, soon after the wedding.

Henry VIII
his marriage to Catherine was planned by Henry VII.

Margaret
m. James IV of Scotland. England and Scotland made peace in 1503.

■ Draw a strip cartoon showing how Henry VII made himself a strong king, making pictures about the following: The Battle of Bosworth, Henry's marriage, Perkin Warbeck, the nobles, money, Henry's death. ◁③▭

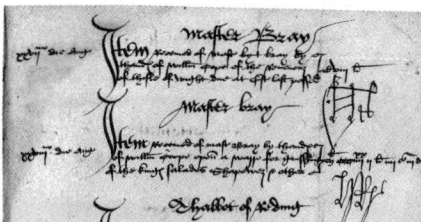

Henry looked after his accounts very carefully. For most of his reign he personally signed every entry with his initial: HR (Henricus Rex, Latin for Henry the King). These two entries show where he decided to change his initial, probably so he could do it faster, without taking his pen off the paper. Copy the two initials carefully, and see whether you find the second one quicker to do. (You may need to practise.) Then design your own initial to use on your possessions – or accounts!

Evidence about Henry VII

Some entries from Henry VII's accounts in 1497

Note When a place is mentioned it shows where the King was. Otherwise he was in London.

7 January	To a little maiden that danceth	£12		
	To a Welshman that maketh rhymes		6s	8d
17 February	To the Queen's fiddler in reward	£1	6s	8d
	To the gardener at Sheen for graftes (cuttings from plants)	£2		
17 March	Sent to the north	£4000		
13 May	Sent to the north	£6300		
31 May	Delivered to the Queen's grace for jewels	£31	10s	
23 June	At the Tower: to one that took Lord Audley	£1		
1 July	Sent to the north	£12 000		
30 July	At Woodstock: for 16 pairs of gloves		5s	4d
10 August	To him that found the new isle	£10		
30 August	Sent to the west	£333	6s	8d
	To Jakes Haute for the tennis play	£10		
10 September	Sent to Exeter	£666	13s	4d
25 September	To a man that came from Perkin	£1		
4 October	At Taunton. The King's losses at cards	£9		
5 October	This day came Perkin Warbeck			
3 December	To my lady mother's poet	£3	6s	8d
18 December	To repay loans	£3364		
	To blind Cunningham		13s	4d
	To the ambassador in Spain in reward	£66	15s	

We know that Henry actually sat for this portrait. It was painted in 1505 when he was quite old. What has he chosen to hold? Artists sometimes had to flatter the important people they painted. Do you think this artist has flattered Henry? What words can you think of to describe the impression he makes on you?

Money was all in coins. There were no banks, credit cards, cheques or paper money.
When Henry sent money to distant places, it went in chests, carefully guarded. ← 2

1 Rule out a page in two columns. In one column, copy out the account entries. In the other, write down the events of 1497 from the box in the margin (shorten them) opposite the entries which link to them. Example:

March 17 To the north ... £4000 | Threat of raids by the Scots.

2 Underline all the entries which show money spent on clothes and enjoyment in one colour. Use a different colour for money spent on dealing with rebels or possible invasion. How can you tell that Henry was more worried about the Scots than Perkin?

3 Why do you think there was a Welsh poet at court (7 January)?

4 What kind of people might the following be:
a) the man that came from Perkin (25 September)?
b) blind Cunningham (18 December)?

5 What did the king spend on December 18 which shows he must have felt fairly confident?

6 Choose an entry that you find interesting or puzzling, and discuss it with your teacher. (Note the amounts Henry spends.)

Some important events in 1497

- James IV had just invaded the north of England for a time. It looked as if he might do it again.
- In Cornwall there was a rebellion against taxes. Some rebels marched to London. Their leader was Lord Audley. Henry attacked them. Lord Audley was captured and executed. 2000 rebels were killed.
- The explorer John Cabot returned from discovering the island he called 'New-Found-Land', near the coast of North America.
- Perkin Warbeck landed in Cornwall. Henry soon captured him.

The handsome prince: Henry VIII (1509–47)

Everyone was delighted with the new young king, Henry VIII. He seemed to have everything. This is what the ambassador from Venice wrote about him a few years after he had become king:

> His Majesty is twenty-nine years old and extremely handsome . . . He is a great deal handsomer than the King of France; very fair, and his whole frame admirably proportioned . . . he has a beard that looks like gold. He is . . . a good musician, composes well, is a most capital horseman, a find jouster, speaks good French, Latin and Spanish, is very religious . . . he is very fond of hunting . . . he is extremely fond of tennis, at which game it is the prettiest thing in the world to see him play, his fair skin glowing through a shirt of the finest texture.

■ Make a list of all the things which the ambassador says Henry is good at doing. (Look below to find out about jousting.) What gets left out, that you might expect a king to spend time doing? ◁1◁

This is the last suit of jousting armour made for Henry, when he was nearly 50. The waist measures 138 centimetres. There is a suit of armour in the Tower of London which the King wore as a young man – waist 82 centimetres!

Jousting was a dangerous sport. It took place in a 'tiltyard' like the one in this picture. The heavily armed knight on horseback thundered down on his opponent on the other side of the barrier, and tried to knock him off his horse with a lance (a long spear).

Henry VIII married Catherine of Aragon as soon as he became king. He said he was obeying his father's dying wish. The queen was five years older than he was, but it was a happy marriage at first. She was sensible and pretty, and a good influence on him. The scene above shows Henry jousting, with Queen Catherine watching him. They are celebrating the birth of their son – but sadly, the baby prince soon died.

1 How can you tell this knight is Henry, and he is jousting in honour of his wife? (*Clue* Catherine was often spelt with a K.) ◁1◁

2 Why is Henry's armour heavier on the left arm and shoulder? ◁1◁

3 Draw a plan of a tiltyard (include the place for the spectators), with labels which explain jousting. ◁3◁

The great cardinal

Henry was interested in so many things that he did not have much time for the ordinary day-to-day business of running the country. Luckily for him he found someone who was ready to do it for him, and to serve him loyally.

Thomas Wolsey began life as the son of a butcher – and in the end he was the most powerful man in England after the King. He became a churchman so he could get a good education, meet people who might help him – and climb to the top. The ladder on the right shows how he did it. He was an energetic, efficient man who loved being rich – he held so many top jobs when he was serving the King that he was richer than any of the nobles at Henry's court. You can imagine what they thought of that, and of the huge palace Wolsey built for himself at Hampton Court.

There is a famous description of how Wolsey went every day to hear law cases in Westminster Hall when he was Lord Chancellor. He wore the red silk robes of a cardinal, and he rode a mule draped in crimson velvet, with gold stirrups. A great procession rode in front of him. He obviously loved every minute of it.

He also worked hard for the King, and did a lot to see that the law courts worked fairly. But neither Henry nor he were as good at managing money as Henry VII had been. So there were more taxes, which nobody liked – and Wolsey was blamed.

Opinions about Wolsey

A The ambassador from Venice thought he did a good job:

> He alone runs all state affairs . . . he has the reputation of being extremely just: he favours the people exceedingly, and especially the poor.

B It was said that when Wolsey went out in the streets, he held a pomander (an orange stuck with cloves) to his nose to keep away the smells of the common people.

C Polydore Vergil was a writer who hated Wolsey – not surprisingly, as Wolsey had once put him in prison. He said:

> Wolsey with his *arrogance* and *ambition* aroused against himself the hatred of the whole country, and by his *hostility* to the nobility and the common people caused them the greatest irritation through his *vainglory*.

1 Look up the words *in italics* first. Do you think that it is possible to believe both **A** and **C**? Explain your answer.

2 **B** may or may not be true. If stories like this get around, are they useful to historians?

3 Henry VIII employed Wolsey for 16 years. Explain in your own words why Wolsey was so useful to the King.

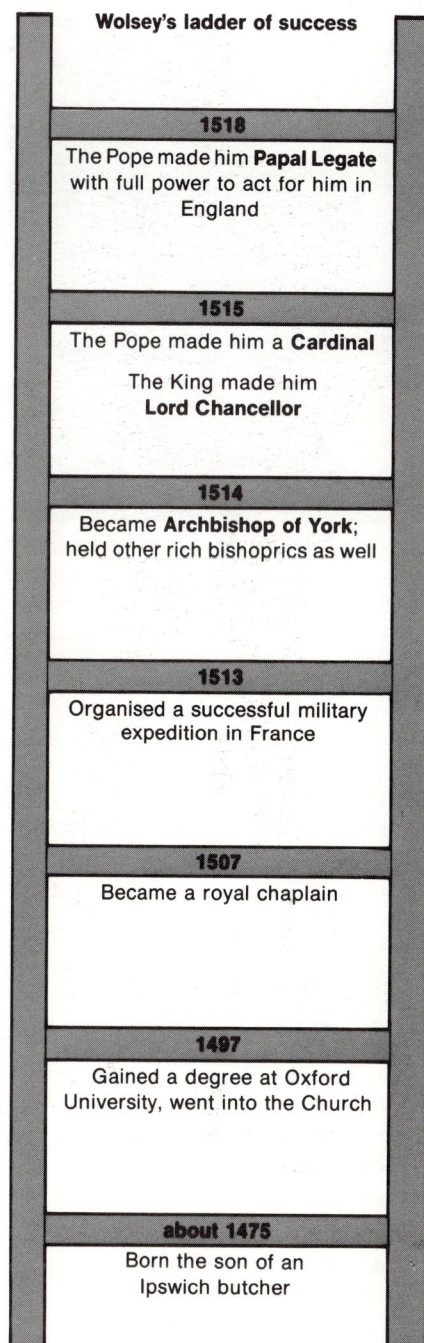

Wolsey's ladder of success

1518
The Pope made him **Papal Legate** with full power to act for him in England

1515
The Pope made him a **Cardinal**

The King made him **Lord Chancellor**

1514
Became **Archbishop of York**; held other rich bishoprics as well

1513
Organised a successful military expedition in France

1507
Became a royal chaplain

1497
Gained a degree at Oxford University, went into the Church

about 1475
Born the son of an Ipswich butcher

Shipwreck!

Right at the beginning of his reign, Henry VIII began to build great warships. The second largest ship he built was the *Mary Rose*, named after his younger sister. (He called the biggest ship after himself.) Henry was proud of his navy, and the *Mary Rose* was one of his most important ships.

A bell found on the Mary Rose, *used to ring for the watch (page 32). The writing round the top is in Latin. It says 'I was made in 1510.'*

This picture of the Mary Rose *comes from a list of the King's ships made in his reign. She bristled with guns – 91 of them. Along her sides she had rows of gunports (holes with lids over them to keep the water out). When the ship went into battle, the crew opened the gunports, and pushed forward the guns so they were ready to fire, as they are in this picture. You can see how close some of the gunports are to the water.*

Some objects found in the *Mary Rose*

The bones of the men who died. The skeleton of a small dog, near a skeleton of a rat it was chasing. The skeleton of a frog
Tudor flies, beetles and cockroaches

Guns of different sizes
Longbows ← 36 and arrows (one box contained 1248 arrows)
Beef, venison and mutton bones cut into serving portions
Plum stones
Peas in the pod
Herbs and spices
Plates and leather bottles
The surgeon's medicine chest full of tools, medicines and bandages ← 1
The surgeon's velvet cap
A pair of fashionable kneelength boots
Shoes
Knitted stockings
Leather jerkins

Trumpet
Tabors (like a recorder)
Pieces of stringed instruments
A backgammon board and pieces
Dice

■ Copy out the groups of objects, giving each group a heading. Draw the ones illustrated, and write underneath how these were probably used.

On 19 July 1545, a French invasion fleet approached Portsmouth. Henry VIII stood watching proudly on the shore, as his fleet sailed out from Portsmouth harbour to attack the French ships. It was a calm, sunny day. The *Mary Rose* was crammed full, with about 600 soldiers and 100 sailors on board. Her gunports were open and her 91 guns were ready to fire. Suddenly, as the sails were going up, the great ship heeled over to one side. Water poured through her gunports and she capsized. She sank so quickly that only about 40 men managed to escape. The King could hear the cries of the drowning soldiers and sailors from the shore. By his side the wife of the commander, Lady Carew, fell in a dead faint as she saw her husband's ship go down.

For over 400 years, the *Mary Rose* lay under water, deep in the mud of the Solent. In 1971, a team of diver archaeologists found her. For 11 difficult years they worked under water, recording and measuring everything they found. They brought up as much as they could. Finally in 1982, a huge crane hauled up the actual ship. Now the ship, and the things found in her, are on display in the *Mary Rose* Museum in Portsmouth. There, you can find out far more than can be fitted on to these two pages about this moment in Tudor time, when the *Mary Rose* sank in July 1545.

More evidence on the *Mary Rose*

Why did she sink?

A The Admiral who commanded the French invasion fleet wrote:

> It was ordered that at daybreak the *galleys* [big armed rowing boats] should advance upon the English . . . The weather favoured our attempt for it was . . . a perfect calm . . . Our galleys had all the advantage of working we could desire, to the great damage of the English who for want of wind lay exposed to our cannon . . . the *Mary Rose*, one of their principal ships, was sunk by our cannon and of 5 or 600 men which were on board, only 5 and 30 escaped.

B A description by an English eye-witness, Sir Peter Carew, brother of the commander of the *Mary Rose*. He had been on board with the King, and returned to shore just before she sailed:

> Sir George Carew [the commander] commanded every man to take his place and the sails to be hoist but . . . no sooner done . . . the *Mary Rose* began to heel, that is to lean over to one side . . . Then [another commander sailing by] called out to Sir George Carew asking him how he did, who answered he had the sort of knaves whom he could not rule, and it was not long after that the said *Mary Rose*, thus heeling more and more, was drowned with 700 men which were in her, with very few escaped.

1 What reason does the French account **A** give for the sinking of the *Mary Rose*? ◁1▱

2 What did Sir George Carew mean when he said he 'had the sort of knaves he could not rule'? ◁1▱

3 How did Sir Peter Carew in **B** think the *Mary Rose* sank? ◁1▱

4 How much do **A** and **B** differ over the numbers on board? Which account is more likely to be right? ◁1▱

5 The archaeologists did not find anything on board to prove the French account. What might they have found if it was true? Why did the French admiral give this account of the sinking? ◁1▱

6 Why do you think the *Mary Rose* sank? ◁4▱

More objects found on the Mary Rose. *Officers usually carried embroidered leather pouches or purses in which they kept their special belongings. This pouch has the initials IHS on it – the Christian sign for Jesus. The other objects are a comb with fine teeth for getting rid of lice, a wooden seal, a pocket sundial, a die, a thimble ring, a decorated clasp, two coins or tokens, a wooden whistle and a rosary.*

1 Which object probably tells us the year the Mary Rose was built? Explain how it was used. ◂ 28 ◁1▱

2 You are a sailor on board the *Mary Rose*. Choose ten different objects from the list and photographs. Explain why they are on your ship. ◂ 28 ◁2▱

3 People often call the *Mary Rose* a time capsule. What do they mean? Make a list of objects which might be found in the wreck of a late twentieth-century ship. Explain what these objects would tell a historian 400 years in the future about our lives. ◁1▱

James IV of Scotland (1488–1513)

Scotland was a separate country from England, and wanted to stay that way. The Scots and the English did not think much of each other, and the border between the two countries was a wild place where both sides raided and stole from one another.

The marriage between James IV and Henry VII's daughter Margaret ← 38 was supposed to make peace, so that England and Scotland were friendly allies. For a time it did.

James IV was an interesting man. See what you think about him.

An opinion of James IV

The Spanish ambassador (but be careful; he was a great friend of James. He was writing before James married Margaret, and was trying to persuade the King of Spain that James should marry one of his daughters. The ambassador wanted to do his own career good too):

> He is of noble stature . . . and as handsome in complexion and shape as a man can be . . . His knowledge of languages is wonderful. He fears God and says all his prayers . . . I have seen him undertake the most dangerous things in the last wars . . . His deeds are as good as his words.

Facts about James IV

- He was only 16 when he became king, but he got control of his wild and independent nobles.
- He encouraged trade, and the country became richer.
- He helped the first Scottish printer, Andrew Miller, to start his printing business in Edinburgh.
- He was interested in medicine, and could set a broken leg and pull out a tooth.
- He made a law saying everyone who was rich enough to own land must send their sons to school. We do not know how it worked – but there were no laws like that in England.

Tradesmen had their own marks which they used on their goods. Andrew Miller (old spelling: Myllar), the first printer in Edinburgh, was already a successful businessman. Find two clues in his trade mark which tell you what his original trade was.

James spent his money on

- jousting tournaments, jugglers, clowns and musicians and poets.
- an inventor John Damien who tried to fly with artificial wings to France off the walls of Stirling Castle. But Damien fell and broke his leg.
- a surgeon to look after a sailor who fell from the rigging of one of James' ships, and a boy injured in one of James' kitchens.
- help for the poor, and for prayers to be said.
- building Holyrood Palace in Edinburgh.
- two big warships, the *Margaret* and the *Great Michael*. (The Margaret cost over £10 000. James' income for a year was £30 000).
- cannons – including a very big one called 'Mons Meg'.

The Battle of Flodden

In 1513, Henry VIII went to war against France, England's old enemy. He did it to impress everyone by winning battles. James saw his chance to do the same thing – and cause trouble for Henry. The Scottish King sent his great warships to sea, and led an invasion army over the border into England, with his big cannon 'Mons Meg'. (Cannon were becoming a much more dangerous weapon by now.) But at Flodden an English army cut the Scots to pieces. Ten thousand Scottish soldiers died. The town of Selkirk had sent a company of spearmen. Only one returned. Thirteen earls were killed, and James' dead body was found under a heap of corpses.

It was a disaster for Scotland. James' son was only two and his widow, Margaret Tudor, had to try to rule the country. The marriage had not brought peace for long.

1 From the way James spent his money, what kind of person do you think he was?

2 Choose words from this list that you think describe James well. Give a reason each time for the word you have chosen.

cowardly	rash	lazy	interested in learning
brave	kind	active	interested in experiments
weak	fun-loving	bored	

3 When you have done that, decide whether you think the Spanish ambassador flattered James – or was probably right about him.

Key words in this section to help you remember and understand what you have learnt. You should be able to use these words now and find evidence in the chapter which illustrates each of them

Henry VI and Edward IV
Lancastrians
Yorkists
court
taxes
royal
queen
gunpowder
cannon
siege
archers
longbows

Princes in the Tower
coronation
heir
murder
suspicion
mystery
motive

Henry VII
nobles
pretenders
rebellion
fines
taxes
accounts
initial

Henry VIII
ambassador
musician
composer
learned
real tennis
hunting
jousting
tiltyard
lance

Wolsey
Cardinal
Chancellor
ambition
procession
pomander

Mary Rose
warship
gunports
capsize
archaeologist
diver
time capsule

James IV
marriage
ally
independence
invasion

4 Crown and Church

Do you need to be told that this is Henry VIII? He is not wearing a crown, but how do you know all the same that you are looking at a powerful king? This is a man who expects to get what he wants. There will be trouble for people who do not obey him.

Henry VIII had always got what he wanted – except for one thing. By 1527, when he had been king for nearly 20 years, he still had no son. He and most of his subjects believed that only a man could rule the country properly.

Henry decided that as Catherine of Aragon had not given him a son, God did not approve of his marriage. He should never have married his brother's widow. ← 38

There seemed to be a simple answer. The Pope must give Henry a divorce so that he could marry again. His Chancellor, Cardinal Wolsey, must get it for him. Henry could think of little else. He called the divorce his 'Great Matter'.

The artist Hans Holbein did this life-size drawing of Henry VIII in 1537, when the King was over 40. But he probably looked like this ten years earlier, at the time of the divorce problem.

The drawing was a pattern for part of a huge wall-painting in full colour, which probably went over Henry's throne in Whitehall Palace. The Palace was burnt down in 1698, but we still have this drawing on canvas and paper – over 400 years old. Henry was pleased with his picture, as it was the image he liked people to have of him. It was copied many times. That is why we all know that Henry looked like this.

■ Try turning the portrait of Henry VIII into a diagram based on two squares, one for the head, the other for the body, with two solid legs. Then if you add the face and clothes, you will have your own portrait of the powerful king. Write some sentences describing him underneath your portrait.

The King's Great Matter

Catherine of Aragon

Catherine had been married to Henry for nearly 20 years, and was middle-aged. She had borne Henry several sons but they had all died. One daughter, Mary, was born in 1516. No one expected Catherine to have any more children. People respected her greatly (probably Henry did too), and she was very religious. When Henry suggested divorce, she had only one answer: she was Henry's own true wife, and nothing could alter that. Something else helped her too. Her nephew, the Emperor Charles V, was the most powerful ruler in Europe. He had just taken the Pope prisoner, and only the Pope could give Henry a divorce.

Anne Boleyn

Anne Boleyn was 20. She was clever, lively and fashionable. Henry was deeply in love with Anne. She was determined to be Queen – and not just his mistress. No one thought she was beautiful, but she knew how to make the best of her glossy dark hair and large eyes. What is she wearing that tells us who she is?

Henry did not often bother to write his own letters, but he wrote lots to Anne. Here is part of one:

> I put myself in great distress ... praying to you with all my heart that you will ... [tell] ... me of your whole mind concerning the love between us two ... having been now above one year struck with the dart of love.

He finished the letter by promising to be faithful to her.

1 How can you tell from Henry's letter that he is not yet sure of Anne? Copy the letter in 'old' writing and sign it like Henry did. ⟨1⟩

2 Draw and colour Anne Boleyn's fashionable new head-dress, called a French hood, and Catherine of Aragon's more old fashioned Spanish hood. Underneath their pictures, explain the importance of Catherine and Anne in the story of Henry's divorce. ⟨3⟩

This is the initial Henry often used to sign his letters. He used a French phrase to finish one of his letters to Anne. It means 'Henry looks for no one else but Anne'. And he surrounded the heart and Anne's initials with the royal HR (Henry the King):

H autre (AB) ne cherche R

The end of Wolsey

Anne Boleyn hated Wolsey. Henry was getting more and more impatient with his Chancellor because he had no divorce.

Wolsey did the best he could to make the Pope grant the King's wish. But he got nowhere. In 1529, Henry sent Wolsey off in disgrace to York – to do his job as Archbishop of York, which he had never had time for until now. But Wolsey went on meddling. Henry ordered the old Cardinal to come to London – almost certainly to be executed. Wolsey was already ill. He died on the way.

1 Why would Wolsey be in trouble, whether he got the divorce or not? ⟨4⟩

2 Write a letter from Wolsey in York to the King, begging for mercy. Bring in everything you have done for him. Begin: ⟨2⟩

> Your Grace, I am your most humble servant, and beg for mercy ...

Henry VIII: Supreme head of the Church of England

Henry VIII found two new men to do his will. When Anne Boleyn became pregnant in 1533 he secretly married her – for this child would of course be the son he had wanted for so long. But Anne gave him another daughter – Elizabeth. Henry was bitterly disappointed. Would this wife fail him too? Still, she was young . . .

Thomas Cromwell

Thomas Cromwell was a clever, efficient man who had been a soldier, a lawyer and a merchant. He was probably Protestant. He helped Henry to find a completely different way to get what he wanted. Why bother about the Pope? English churchmen should obey the King, just like all his other subjects. Henry ordered Parliament to pass a law which gave him a grand new title – **the Supreme Head of the Church of England**. All important people had to swear that they accepted Anne Boleyn as Queen. There would be trouble if they refused.

Thomas Cranmer

Thomas Cranmer was a quiet scholar who would probably have liked to spend his life studying. But there was no chance of that, because Henry made him Archbishop of Canterbury. He was a Protestant, but he kept quiet about it. He gave Henry **the divorce** he had wanted for so long. Cranmer seemed to be able to keep out of trouble. He was the only one of Henry's close advisers who did not lose the King's favour.

Sir Thomas More: The King's good servant

Thomas More was a famous scholar, and a successful lawyer. He wrote a best-selling book called *Utopia*. This described an imaginary island where everyone shared all their possessions. No one could be poor, because there was no money. Silver and gold were just children's toys – no adult bothered with them. Everyone wore a plain grey uniform, and worked six hours a day. They shared all the daily tasks and had an equal amount of leisure. Thomas More was probably criticising wealth and selfishness, especially in the Church. He was a very religious man, and nearly became a monk when he was young.

Thomas lived in a big house in Chelsea with a lovely garden and a small zoo. He had a big family, and educated his daughters well (this was unusual). Many interesting visitors came – famous scholars, the artist Hans Holbein, and the king himself all enjoyed his company.

1 Thomas Cromwell wore dark, plain clothes. In the rest of the portrait are his books and writing materials. Write down some words to describe the man you see in this portrait.

2 There are three people called Thomas on these two pages. They all served Henry VIII. Write a short paragraph about each of them. Describe their characters and the work they did for the King.

Henry VIII admired Thomas More. In 1529, when Henry got rid of Wolsey the king made Thomas his Chancellor. Thomas may have accepted the job to try to protect the Church. He had a prison for heretics ← 33 in his garden.

But Thomas did not approve of the King's divorce. He thought the King was wrong to break with the Pope, and make himself head of the Church. In the end he resigned, and refused to swear the oath Henry demanded.

Henry did all he could to make Thomas change his mind. He was imprisoned in a small damp cell in the Tower. His family were forced to go and plead with him to give in. His books were taken away. He was questioned many times. But for 17 months, Thomas More remained silent. Eventually he was put on trial and executed. Before he died, he said:

I die the King's good servant, but God's servant first.

This is a very unusual picture because it is like a modern snapshot. The people are not thinking about how the artist will draw them, and they are not trying to look their best. Holbein shows Thomas More and his family just as they are getting ready for family prayers. They are opening their prayer books, and have left other books scattered on the floor.

Find: Thomas (he is in the middle, wearing a chain which shows he is an important servant of the King), his old father, his wife (kneeling at a small desk, with a monkey nestling in her skirts), his son, a servant standing by the door (and two outside), five daughters (two are adopted). What else can you see?

1 In *Utopia* there is an imaginary map. Draw your own imaginary map of a perfect island. Make it into a poster which explains what life is like on your island – work, homes, family life, holidays, money. ◁4▷

2 Make your own strip cartoon of the life and death of Thomas More. ◁3▷

The end of the monasteries

The English Church had been part of the Catholic Church, under the Pope, for nearly a thousand years. That stopped when Henry VIII made himself Supreme Head. But so far he had not touched a very big part of the English Church – the monasteries and nunneries, over 800 of them. They still obeyed the Pope. They were also very rich. They probably owned about a quarter of the land of England, and a great deal of treasure too. Many of them had relics – objects said to be the remains of saints. People travelled from a long way to see relics, and to pray that they might help them. Often the monastery would do very well out of these 'tourists'. Hailes Abbey in Gloucestershire had a tiny jar of the 'Holy Blood of Christ'. A Protestant who disapproved wrote in 1533:

> You would wonder to see how they came by flocks out of the west country . . . chiefly to the Blood of Hailes.

You can see the jobs that monks and nuns were often supposed to do in the diagram. Some did not do them very well – but some helped people a lot.

Henry decided to get rid of the monasteries for two reasons:
- Monks and nuns might obey the Pope and not him.
- He was short of money.

Nuns and monks were expected to go to church eight times during each 24 hours – day and night. These nuns are singing in their convent church. They have three big knots in their girdles to remind them of the three vows all nuns and monks made: poverty – to give up their possessions and stay in the monastery; chastity – to have nothing to do with the opposite sex; and obedience – to obey the abbot or abbess without question.

Monks and nuns
- provided a priest for the village
- ran schools
- helped the poor
- looked after travellers
- cared for the sick

Thomas Cromwell's investigation

Henry told his chief adviser to do the job. First Cromwell needed to 'prove' that monks and nuns were not doing their job properly. He sent round officials to ask lots of questions. They were expected to get the right kind of answers.

Questions and answers

Some questions asked by Cromwell's men: Do you attend the right number of church services? Do you stay in the monastery all the time? Can you read and write? Do you overeat?

■ Work out some other questions which must have been asked, from this report to Cromwell on the abbey of Bury St Edmund's, Suffolk:

As for the abbot, we found nothing suspect about his living, but . . . he lay forth much in his *granges* [houses owned by the abbot, separate from the monastery], that he delighted much in playing at dice and cards, and therein spent much money . . . and there was much frequence of women coming to the monastery . . . Among the relics we found . . . the coals that St Lawrence was toasted, the paring of St Edmund's nails, and *skills* [magic spells] for the headache.

Stones from the walls
Bells from the tower
Lead from the roof
Treasures from the church
Land belonging to the monastery

A modern photograph of the ruins of Rievaulx Abbey in Yorkshire.

■ Make a list of the labelled items, and say what probably happened to them. (Use the information on this page.) ◁3〰

Cromwell's investigation found plenty wrong, though his officials may have made some of it up. The King had what he wanted – the excuse to destroy all the monasteries in England. He took the land and everything valuable. In the north, many people joined a rebellion called the Pilgrimage of Grace, partly to try to save the monasteries. Henry crushed it ruthlessly. But on the whole the monks and nuns went quietly. Monks often became local priests. Nuns had a harder time. They got lower pensions than monks and Henry forbade them to marry – but what else could they do?

Cromwell hoped that Henry would now have enough money to run the country. But the King went on spending so much that he had to sell most of the land to his nobles and other landowners. They did very well out of the monasteries. They did not want to see them back.

What happened at Hailes Abbey, Gloucestershire

Removed by Cromwell's men: 'jewels, plate (silver and gold objects) ornaments and money'.

The 'Holy Blood' of Hailes was examined in London and declared to be 'honey clarified and coloured with saffron, as has been evidently proved before the King and his Council'.

The abbot had a pension of £100 a year.

The monks got pensions from £8 to £1 6s a year

In 1542, Richard Andrews, a landowner and businessman, bought the land, and probably pulled down the abbey church. Later, the rest of the buildings were used as farmhouses and barns. Local people probably took much of the stone. There is only a ruin there today.

What the King took from St Osyth's Abbey in Essex

261 wagonloads of lead, from several buildings including the steeple and roof of the church	£1044
Treasure, including a silver gilt crown for the skull of St Osyth, a famous relic	£175 18s 6d
Corn, cattle, household goods	£250
Bells	£40

1 What is the most valuable item the King got from St Osyth's? ◁1〰

2 How can you tell that St Osyth's was an important monastery with several big buildings? ◁1〰

3 Look at the information opposite. How much did the end of the monasteries probably affect the lives of ordinary people? ◁4〰

4 Divide into groups of about ten. Half of each group decide what questions Cromwell's men will ask when they investigate a monastery, or convent. The other half decide what sort of answers the monks or nuns will give, and what happens to them. (Do not make things all bad.) Get together and use what you have worked out to write and act a play about the end of a monastery. It could be Hailes Abbey – or perhaps one near your school. ◁2〰

51

The Bible in English

In 1539, Henry VIII allowed the first official translation of the Bible into English to be printed. This was a big step, because Protestants believed that everyone should be able to read the Bible in their own language. But Henry was not a Protestant. He just wanted to run the English Church instead of the Pope. He made sure everyone realised he was in control of the Church when they saw the first page. Look at it carefully.

The picture on the first page of the English Bible was carefully planned. At the top, the King sits on his throne handing out Bibles to his most important subjects. It is rather difficult to find God, but he is there, above Henry's head. Below the King, Cranmer (in his Archbishop's mitre) and Cromwell hand out Bibles too. At the bottom a preacher tells ordinary people to pray for all men, especially the King. They all answer (in Latin) 'Long live the King.' Pick out as many things as you can which show this picture is more about Henry's power than about reading the Bible.

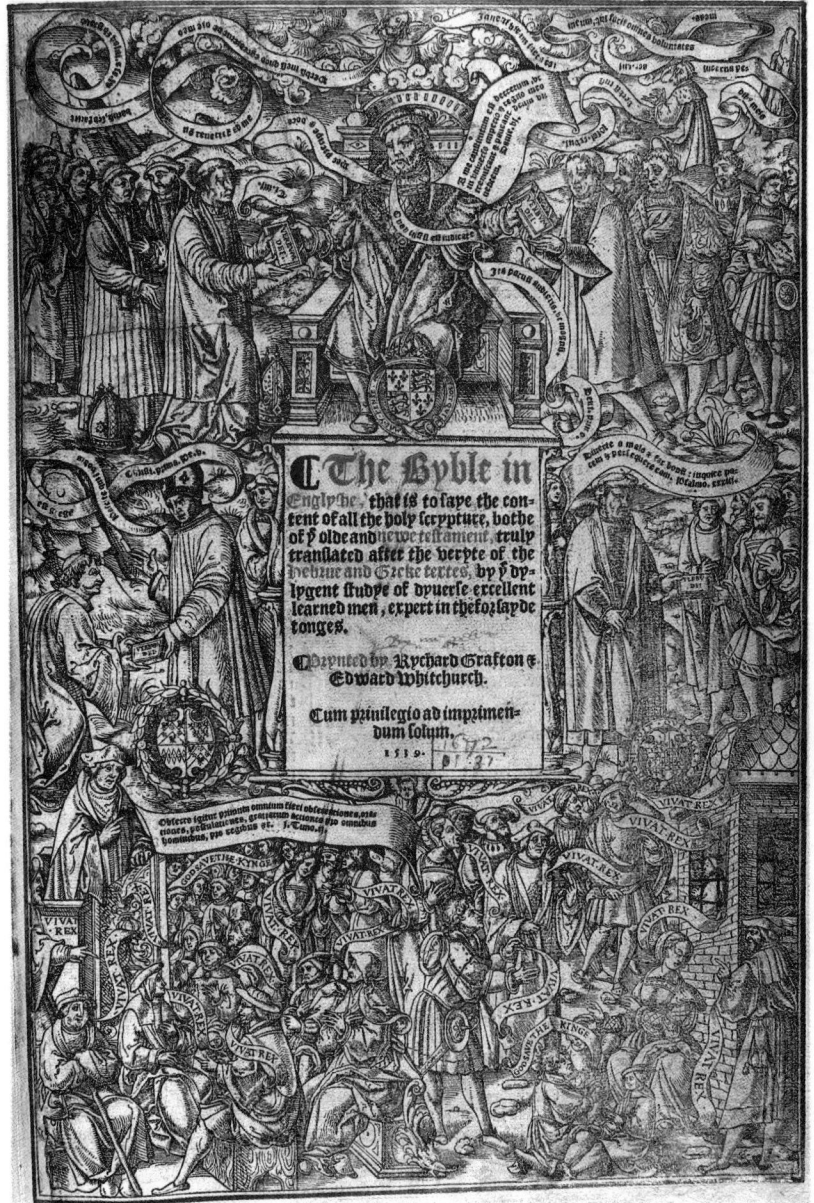

1 Choose three of the statements below to complete the following sentence sensibly:

Henry VIII's law about Bible reading is evidence that

- only rich men could read.
- more ordinary people were learning to read.
- printed books were expensive.
- printed books were reasonably cheap.
- rich people were worried that Bible reading might make ordinary people think for themselves too much, and cause trouble.

2 Laws telling people what to read usually do not work. Why not?

Henry soon had second thoughts about letting everyone read the Bible. He ordered Parliament to pass a law forbidding 'women, apprentices, . . . serving men and labourers' to read it, because 'it was disputed, rhymed, sung and jangled in every alehouse'. But it was too late. More and more people read the English Bible. It became one of the most important books in the English language.

Jane Seymour.   Anne of Cleves.   Katherine Parr.

Four more wives

Anne Boleyn did become pregnant again. But the son she carried was born dead. Henry was getting tired of her sharp tongue anyway. In 1536 he accused her of being unfaithful. Almost certainly this was not true. But she was found guilty and beheaded – with a sword, not an axe, as a sign of 'mercy'.

Jane Seymour was a quiet, rather plain girl at court. Perhaps Henry liked that after Anne's nagging. He married Jane 11 days after Anne's execution. Jane had the son Henry had wanted for so long – **Edward**, born 1537. But she died 12 days later.

Anne of Cleves was a German princess. In 1540, Cromwell persuaded Henry to make an alliance with some German Protestant princes. But Henry was not very keen – even less keen when he saw Anne. He apparently said she looked like a horse. He divorced her straight away. It was the end of Cromwell too. He was executed soon after.

Catherine Howard was young and attractive (though we have no portrait of her). Henry married her in 1540, as soon as his divorce was rushed through. He was unhealthy and overweight by now. Catherine had a lover . . . and Henry found out. In 1542 she was executed.

Katherine Parr was a sensible widow. Henry married her in 1543, and she looked after him and his three children. The King died in 1547. Katherine survived him.

1 Make a table showing what happened to Henry VIII's six wives, with columns headed like this:

Name of wife	Date of marriage	How long was she Queen?	Children? (born when?)	What happened to her?

Find the information you need on pages 40 and 46–8, as well as here.

2 Write down Henry's children in order of age. Put how old they were in 1547, when Henry died.
Then write down the order in which they would become the next ruler. It should be different. Why?

3 You are a reporter interviewing Henry VIII at the end of his reign. What questions would you like to ask him? How do you think he would answer them? If possible, act out the interview in class and tape or video it.

Henry VIII at the end of his life, when he was old and very overweight. He had a bad ulcer on his leg which, it was said, sometimes made him go black in the face with agony. A special machine hauled him up and down-stairs when he could not walk. Compare this picture with the one of Henry on page 46.

53

Edward VI: The Protestant king

Edward VI, Henry's only son, was nine years old when he became king. This picture was painted at the beginning of his reign, and of course it is a made-up scene. It is Protestant propaganda – it was painted to put over Protestant ideas. Although Edward was young, he was a firm Protestant and so were the people who ruled for him.

In the picture, Henry VIII is on his deathbed and he is passing on his power to his son. On the right are Edward's council (advisers). Edward's uncle, the Duke of Somerset, stands beside him. He ruled for Edward, but he did not make a success of it. Next to the Duke of Somerset is John Dudley, who took power from him and became the Duke of Northumberland. Archbishop Cranmer is there too. In Edward's reign, he became openly Protestant, and wrote the first English Prayer Book. Right under the King is the Pope. The English Bible is landing hard on his head, doing him no good at all. Catholic monks on the left escape fast. In the top right-hand corner, soldiers pull down a statue of the Virgin Mary. Protestants did not approve of Catholic statues.

1 Explain why this is a made-up scene, which could not have actually happened.

2 How does the picture tell you that Edward is the king, although he is only a boy?

3 Make labelled sketches of things in the picture which tell you that Edward and his council were Protestant. ← 32, 33

The Tudor Family

HENRY VII (1485–1509) m. ELIZABETH OF YORK

- Arthur (d. 1502) m. Catherine of Aragon
- HENRY VIII (1509–47) m.
  - 1 Catherine of Aragon
  - 2 Anne Boleyn
  - 3 Jane Seymour
  - 4 Anne of Cleves
  - 5 Catherine Howard
  - 6 Catherine Parr

  - MARY I (1553–8) m. Philip of Spain
  - ELIZABETH I (1558–1603)
  - EDWARD VI (1547–53)

- Margaret m. JAMES IV of Scotland (1488–1513)
  - JAMES V (1513–42) m. Mary of Guise
    - Mary, Queen of Scots (Mary Stuart) (1542–67)
      - JAMES VI of Scotland and I of England (1567–1625) The Stuart line begins in 1603.

- Mary m. Duke of Suffolk
  - Frances m. Henry Grey
    - Lady Jane Grey "The Nine Day's Queen" (1553)

REIGNING SOVEREIGNS ARE IN CAPITAL LETTERS
The dates of their reigns are shown by their names

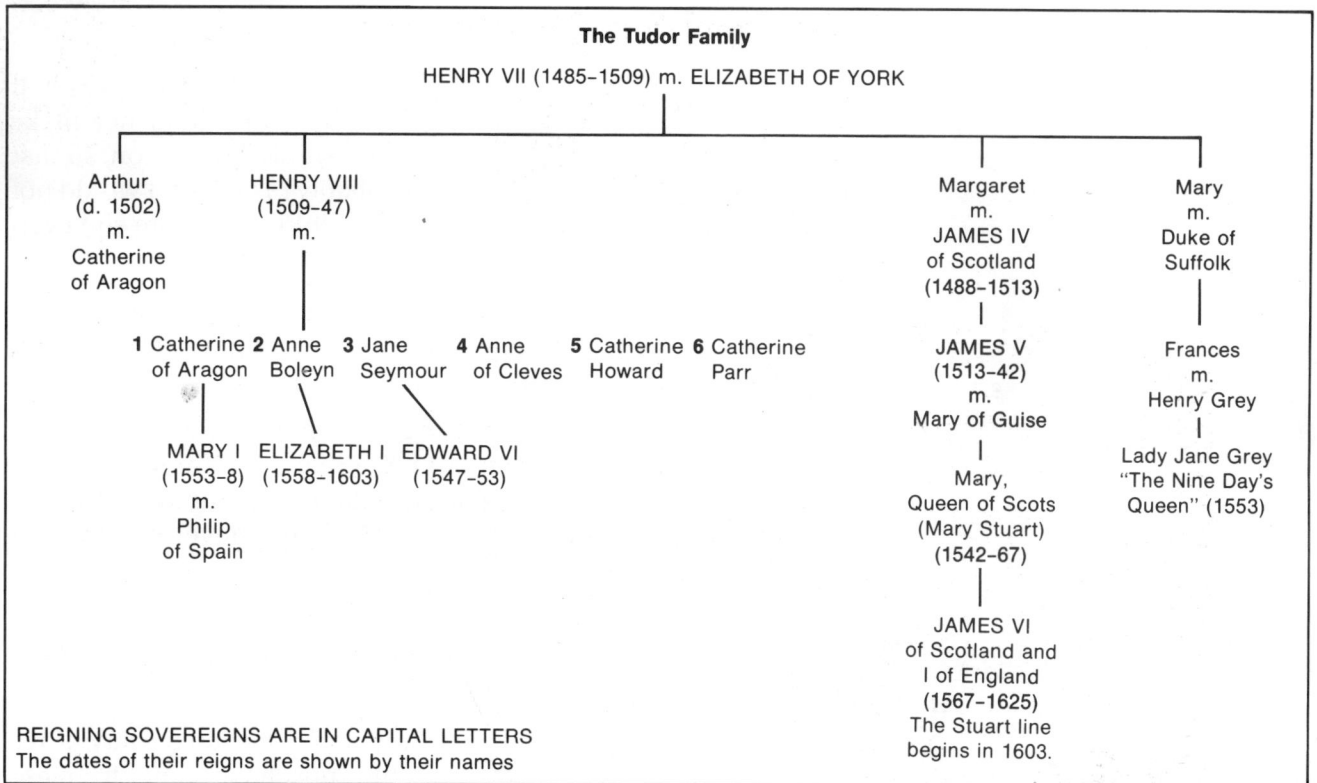

A queen to rule

Although Henry VIII did everything he could to make sure he had a son to follow him, soon a Queen ruled the country after all, for the first time for hundreds of years.

Edward became very ill with tuberculosis and died when he was 16. He wanted a Protestant to follow him, and so did some of his councillors. They tried to make his cousin Lady Jane Grey Queen. But almost everyone wanted the rightful Queen – Henry VIII's eldest daughter Mary.

This picture shows Mary at the beginning of her reign. She was 37, and probably looked older. She had a hard life. She was 12 when Henry VIII divorced Catherine of Aragon. She never saw her mother again, but she was very loyal to her and was a firm Catholic. In Edward VI's reign, she had refused to become Protestant. Now she wanted one thing above all – to make England Catholic again.

Everyone thought Mary should marry as soon as possible, so her husband could help her rule. But this husband would be very powerful, so there was a problem. If the Queen married an English nobleman, other powerful nobles would be jealous. And if she married a foreign ruler, England would probably be tied to a foreign country.

■ Look at the chart you made of Henry VIII's wives. If Mary had no children, who would be the next ruler? ← 53

The Spanish marriage

Mary decided to marry Philip of Spain. Remember she was half Spanish. ←[38] She believed that Philip could help her make England Catholic again. She hoped she would have a son, so that her half-sister Elizabeth (who was probably Protestant) would not be the next queen. Mary was in love with Philip before she even saw him.

The marriage only brought her sadness. Many English people did not like having their Queen married to a foreigner. There was a rebellion even before Philip arrived for the wedding.

Philip was ten years younger than Mary, and only agreed to marry her because he thought it might help Spain. He soon went back there, leaving Mary lonely and miserable. She thought she was pregnant. But in fact she was seriously ill and never had the son she longed for so much.

Philip dragged England into a war against France. Calais was lost – the last English possession in Europe. Everyone, including Mary, felt this was a terrible disgrace.

Mary had very little time – her reign only lasted five years. She did not have time to make England Catholic again. She would have liked to bring back the monasteries. Why did the powerful ruling classes who owned land make that difficult? ←[51]

Like many religious people then, Mary believed she should punish those who disagreed with her, because this would save them from Hell. So anyone who was Protestant was in danger. Richer Protestants escaped to Protestant countries in Europe. But about 300 people were burnt because of their Protestant beliefs.

The North
of England

East Anglia

Wales   The Midlands

Gloucester-
shire   Oxford   Herts Essex
Middlesex

London
Kent

Sussex

Devon

Cornwall

Places where Protestants were burnt
- London 46   • Middlesex 13   • Essex 52
- Kent 59   • Sussex 27   • Hertfordshire 3
- East Anglia 35   • Gloucestershire 10
- Oxford 3   • Midlands 14   • Wales 3
- Devon and Cornwall 1   • North of England 1

People burnt
Mainly weavers, clothworkers and shopkeepers, including more than 50 women.
Also 4 bishops and 16 priests.

1 Copy the map, and put the numbers of people burnt in each area in red beside the name of the area.

2 Shade in three colours for
- places where under ten Protestants were burnt
- places with under 20
- places with 20 or over.
Put a key to explain what the colours mean.

3 Under the map make a block graph from the figures.

4 Then write sentences explaining which part of England had most Protestants burnt, and what kind of people these Protestants were.

Protestant martyrs

Martyrs are people who die for their beliefs. This picture comes from John Foxe's *Book of Martyrs*, printed five years after Mary died. It told the stories of the Protestants burnt in Mary's reign. John Foxe was a strong Protestant. He was not in England during Mary's reign, so he could not have been an eye-witness, though we know he talked to people who were there. They were Protestants too – so his book is very biased, though he did not actually make things up. This picture shows the burning of two famous Protestant bishops, Nicholas Ridley and Hugh Latimer, in Oxford.

In the top left-hand corner, Archbishop Cranmer prays for his friends as they face their terrible death. We know that Cranmer was in prison near by, and forced to watch. Catholic friars tried to make him give up his Protestant beliefs. In the end Cranmer gave in, and recanted – he signed a statement saying he was a Catholic. But then he learnt he would be burnt anyway for his past beliefs. He realised what he had done. When he was burnt, he put the hand which had signed into the flames first, crying out 'This hand hath offended.' Then he died bravely.

1 Why did Mary particularly want to punish Cranmer? ← 48, 54

2 Make a strip cartoon of the main events in Cranmer's life, covering three reigns – Henry VIII, Edward VI, Mary I.

3 Foxe's *Book of Martyrs* became a best-seller, and made sure people did not forget the burnings in Mary's reign. How would this picture help them remember? (Remember they had no TV, radio or newspapers.)

4 Do you think Foxe's book is a primary or a secondary source?

The young Elizabeth

Henry VIII's younger daughter had a difficult childhood too. Her mother was beheaded when she was two. Her nurse wrote to Cromwell (perhaps she did not dare write to Henry) saying that the little princess was short of clothes and:

> hath great pain with her great teeth, and they come very slowly forth, and causeth me to suffer Her Grace to have her *will* [way] more than I would [like].

Elizabeth had four stepmothers. The last one, Katherine Parr, looked after her kindly, and Elizabeth lived with her after Henry's death. Elizabeth learnt young that she had to be cautious about people and hide her feelings. In Mary's reign she was sent to the Tower for a time and was in danger of her life, because Mary thought her sister had been involved in the rebellion against the marriage with Philip. Elizabeth was cautious about religion too. It was dangerous *not* to go to Catholic services in Mary's reign, but Elizabeth usually found some excuse – she was often 'not well'! Most people thought Elizabeth was Protestant.

■ Who was Elizabeth's mother? Why would Mary find it difficult to get on with Elizabeth?

This portrait was painted when Elizabeth was 13. She chose to be painted holding a book, to show her learning – and perhaps to show off her long slim hands.

The new queen

The Spanish ambassador was worried when Elizabeth became Queen. He wrote to Philip about her:

> She is much attached to her people, and is very confident they are on her side. . . . She seems to me [very much] more feared than her sister, and gives her orders and has her way as absolutely as her father did.

■ What are the two things the Spanish ambassador says about Elizabeth? He did not like Elizabeth very much, because she refused to take his advice. Does this mean we should not believe what he says? Discuss this with the class.

When Elizabeth became Queen in 1558, she was determined to 'have her way' over religion, because there had been so many confusing changes. She wanted a 'middle way' between Catholic and Protestant – and no more changes. She was lucky. She ruled for over 40 years, so people had time to get used to the new Church of England – though some never accepted it.

The coronation of the young Queen. In this portrait by an unknown artist her red hair flows loose under her crown. She holds the sceptre and orb, the other two symbols of her power.

	CATHOLIC	Changes in the Church	PROTESTANT
HENRY VIII		Henry Supreme Head The end of the Monasteries The English Bible	
EDWARD VI			The English Prayer Book No statues or pictures in church
MARY I		The Pope's power restored Protestants persecuted	
ELIZABETH I	Many Catholics could not accept the new Church of England	THE CHURCH OF ENGLAND • kept bishops and the familiar church buildings • no Pope • no monks or nuns • fewer pictures and statues • the English Bible • services in English **Fines for those who refused to go to church**	Some Protestants thought the Church should be much more Protestant. They were called **Puritans**.

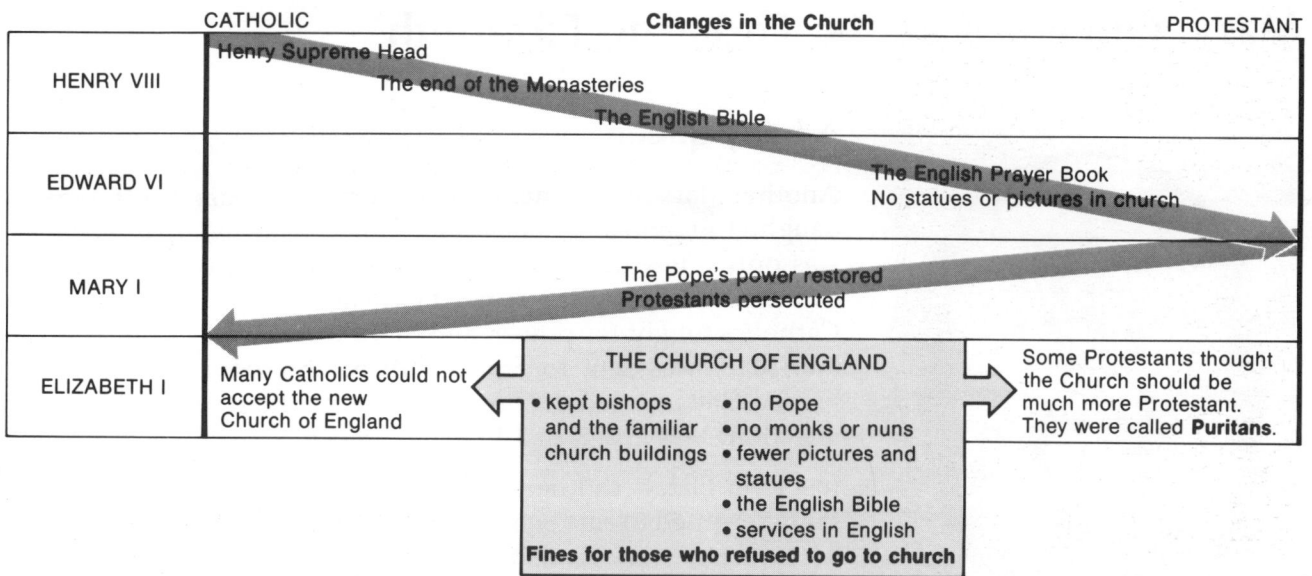

1 Work out where all the people are in the picture. Trace the outline of the picture and label the people.

2 Explain why this must be an imaginary scene, which could not really have taken place.

3 Explain the reason for the position of Mars and the two goddesses.

4 In whose reign must this picture have been painted? Explain your answer.

5 What is the picture saying about the ruler who is on the throne? Is it Catholic or Protestant propaganda?

You have seen some examples of propaganda in this chapter – when words or pictures give a particular viewpoint. This picture is propaganda by the government of England. It is called The Protestant Succession. *It shows Henry VIII, Edward VI, Mary I, Philip of Spain, Elizabeth I and also Mars, the Roman god of war, and two goddesses of peace and plenty.*

Mary, Queen of Scots: Threat to Elizabeth

Mary Queen of Scots was tall, slim and red-haired. People at the time thought she was very beautiful.

A baby queen

Another Mary now comes into the story. This Mary was the grand-daughter of James IV. ← 44 Her father, James V, died when she was only a few days old. Her mother, Mary of Guise, ruled the country for her. It was a difficult time in Scotland. Protestants and Catholics fought for power, and there were attacks from England too. Mary was sent to France, where she grew up. She loved France. She married the French king – but he soon died of an ear infection. Mary then had to leave France.

Just after Elizabeth I became Queen of England, Mary (aged 19) sadly returned to rule Scotland. Elizabeth and Mary were cousins. ← 55 They were rivals too, because:

- If Elizabeth had no children, Mary was her heir.
- Some English Catholics did not accept Henry VIII's marriage with Anne Boleyn. They thought Elizabeth had no right to be Queen of England, and supported Mary.
- Mary was Catholic, Elizabeth was Protestant.

Marriages, murders and rebellion

Mary decided to marry again. She chose Henry Darnley. He was tall and handsome, but also weak, big-headed and drank too much. Mary soon became very unhappy and spent a lot of time with her Italian secretary, David Riccio. Darnley was jealous.

One evening, Darnley and other nobles burst into Mary's room in Holyrood Palace where she was having a supper party. Riccio clung terrified to the Queen's skirts. The nobles dragged him out of the room and stabbed him over 50 times.

Soon after, Mary gave birth to a son, James. She seemed to make it up with Darnley – but she had not forgiven him. She relied more and more on a Protestant noble, the Earl of Bothwell, even though she was a Catholic.

On 9 February 1567, Darnley was staying in a house called Kirk o'Field in Edinburgh. He had been ill, and Mary was looking after him. Late in the evening, Mary left the house to join a wedding party. Darnley was in bed in an upstairs room. In the middle of the night, there was a huge explosion. The house blew up. The bodies of Darnley and his servant were found in the garden. The explosion had not touched them. They had been strangled.

Three months later Mary married Bothwell (he had to divorce his wife first). Everyone thought he had murdered Darnley, but Mary did nothing. Many people were horrified. There was a rebellion, and Mary was taken prisoner. Her baby son James was made King James VI. Bothwell escaped to Denmark and died miserably in prison. Mary finally escaped too – over the border into England.

■ Write about Mary's marriages to Darnley and Bothwell, explaining why each went wrong. (Find three reasons why many of Mary's subjects disapproved of her marriage to Bothwell.)

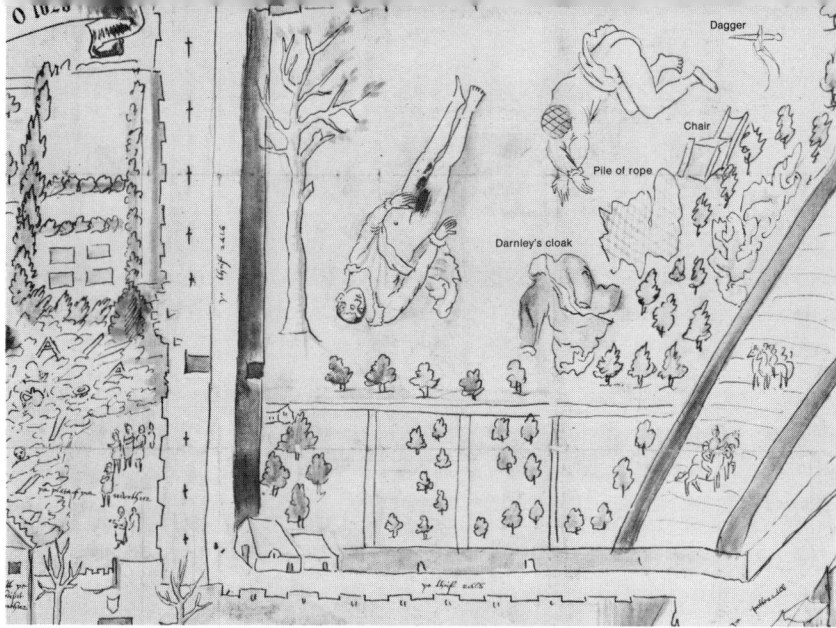

1 No one knows exactly what happened when Darnley died. The four labelled objects by the two bodies may be clues. Write your own story of what might have happened, explaining why those four objects might be there. Begin with these events, and make it exciting! (Remember to include all four objects.)

Darnley wakes suddenly in the middle of the night – looks out of his upstairs window – realises his enemies are outside the house – what are they going to do? – decides he must escape – quickly calls his servant, who grabs the only weapon he can find – a small dagger . . .

2 Make a strip cartoon of the events in Mary's life so far.

What should Elizabeth do with Mary?

Elizabeth's problems:

Mary may have had something to do with Darnley's murder.	➡ Should Elizabeth put her on trial?
Mary was Catholic. She was heir to the English throne.	➡ English Catholics might support her.
She was closely linked to France, who was not friendly to England.	➡ The French might help her.
She was Elizabeth's cousin, and a queen.	➡ Elizabeth felt Mary should be treated like a queen.

Protestant nobles now ruled Scotland for the baby James, and could be useful allies.

Elizabeth could:
- send Mary back to Scotland (what would the rebels do with her?)
- send Mary to France (would the French give her an army?)
- keep Mary in prison in England (would Catholics plot to put her on the throne?)

■ Your class becomes Elizabeth's council. In pairs, work out arguments for and against each of Elizabeth's three choices. Then have a class discussion and vote on what Elizabeth should do with Mary.

Walsingham was one of Elizabeth's most important councillors, and a very strong Protestant. Some historians think he forged part of Mary's letter to Babington, to make sure she was found guilty.

■ Make a Protestant poster demanding the death of Mary Queen of Scots. Call her 'The Monstrous Huge Dragon'. Illustrate it! You will find a good dragon on page 67.

This drawing of Mary's execution was made at the time. Find three scenes in this picture: Mary enters the hall; She stands on the scaffold with her ladies, who take off her black outer dress; She is executed.

The monstrous huge dragon

Elizabeth put Mary in prison in England. In 1570, the Pope ordered English Catholics not to support Elizabeth 'the pretended Queen'. Most English Catholics just wanted to be able to have Catholic services. They did not want to plot against Elizabeth. Should they be loyal to the Pope or to Elizabeth? It was a terrible choice.

Some Catholics did plot to kill Elizabeth and put Mary on the throne. Parliament begged for Mary's execution. They called her a 'monstrous huge dragon'. But for nearly 20 years, Elizabeth refused. She probably did not want to execute another queen.

One of Elizabeth's councillors, Sir Francis Walsingham, set up a spy system to trap the plotters, and Mary too. Walsingham employed a double agent. This spy pretended he was working for Mary. He arranged for her to send and receive letters in code in a leather packet, hidden in beer barrels delivered to Mary's household. But the spy also decoded and copied the letters for Walsingham. Soon some plotters led by a rash young Catholic, Anthony Babington, started to write to Mary. They planned to kill Elizabeth and make Mary Queen. Mary's answer gave Walsingham the evidence he needed. Elizabeth reluctantly agreed that Mary must die.

On a cold February morning in 1587, the local gentry gathered in the great hall of Fotheringay Castle, Northamptonshire, to witness the death of Mary Queen of Scots. Soon after 8 o'clock, Mary entered the crowded hall with her ladies. She wore a black dress with a crimson petticoat, and a white veil on her red hair. She carried a crucifix. She was middle-aged now, and lame with rheumatism, but she was very dignified. She refused to join in with English prayers, and said her own Latin ones loudly and firmly. Her ladies removed her black outer dress. Now she was dressed in crimson from head to toe – the colour of a martyr ←[57]. The executioner had to make two blows to cut off her head. Then he lifted the head to show everyone she was dead. As he did so it fell from his hand – he was left holding a red wig, and the white veil pinned to it. Mary's pet dog crept out from her skirts, and crouched between her head and body, covered with blood.

1 The description of Mary's execution is based on eye-witness accounts. Find as much evidence as you can to show that Mary meant everyone to know that she died as a Catholic martyr. Is the description here primary or secondary evidence? ←[1]

2 Look carefully at the drawing of Mary's execution. Then finish your strip cartoon of her life and death. ←[61]

Traitors or martyrs?

Traitors are people who betray their country. You already know the word martyr. ← 57 About 250 Catholics were executed as traitors in Elizabeth's reign. (How many Protestants died in Mary I's reign? ← 56)

Some Catholics, like Babington, did plot to kill Elizabeth. Many others just wanted to have Catholic services. They needed priests to hold these services. But as the danger from plots grew, there were new laws forbidding Catholic priests to come to England. The punishment for them and those who helped them was death.

By 1580, Catholic priests were coming secretly into England. Some arrived at busy ports disguised as merchants. Others arrived by night on lonely beaches. They were hidden in 'safe houses'. Edmund Campion was one of the first priests to come. He wrote a letter to the priests in Rome who sent him:

> I ride daily in the country, *meditating* my *sermon* on horseback, hear *confession*, and after *Mass*, preach, being greedily heard ... I cannot long escape the *heretics*, they have so many *scouts*. I wear ridiculous clothes, often change my name and so often read newsletters that Campion is taken that I am without fear ... I find many neglecting their own security to have only care of my safety.

1 Make sure you understand the words in *italics*.

2 What evidence is there in this letter that Campion had not come to plot, but to hold services and teach loyal Catholics? (Is he likely to tell the truth in this kind of letter?)

3 How can you tell that he is getting a lot of help from Catholics in spite of the danger?

4 Does Campion think he will be captured? Is he afraid?

5 Make a government poster: WANTED, EDMUND CAMPION, CATHOLIC PLOTTER ... It should have suitable warnings and illustrations, and instructions to report to the Justice of the Peace (usually the local landowner, who had to keep law and order in his area – there were no policemen in Tudor England).

On page 57 you read about the death of a Protestant martyr, Thomas Cranmer. Cranmer and Campion both died bravely for their faith. Protestants and Catholics persecuted each other at this time, and there were terrible religious wars. It was a long time before Christians began to learn toleration – respect for other people's beliefs, even when they are different.

■ What examples can you think of today when people do not show toleration – of other people's religious beliefs, or their cultures and lifestyle?

Campion was finally captured at Lyford Grange, Berkshire, in a hiding place like the one below. He was tortured to make him confess to plotting. He refused. He said: 'I am a Catholic man and a priest. In that faith I have lived hitherto, and in that faith I do intend to die.' He was hanged, drawn and quartered, and just before his death he said firmly that Elizabeth was his 'lawful princess and Queen'. This picture is Protestant propaganda, showing what happens to Catholic priests. It also shows another priest, Robert Parsons, who did plot – and was never captured.

Below is a hiding place for Catholic priests in Sawston Hall, near Cambridge, a Catholic 'safe house'. Priests hid in cramped spaces behind passages, up chimneys or under the floor, sometimes with no food, for several days while soldiers searched the house for them.

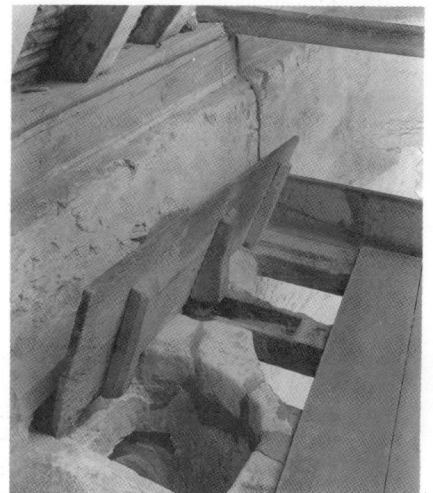

The Spanish Armada, 1588

When Elizabeth became Queen, Philip II of Spain was friendly. After all, he had been married to her sister. He was also ruler of Spain, the strongest Catholic country in Europe. But gradually, Protestant Elizabeth and Catholic Philip became bitter enemies. Religion was not the only reason:

- England began to challenge Spain at sea. Francis Drake and other English seamen attacked Spanish treasure ships bringing gold and silver from the Spanish Empire in America to Spain.
- Philip ruled the Netherlands as well as Spain. English soldiers had been helping the Dutch to fight the strong Spanish army there, commanded by the Duke of Parma.
- Philip was already planning to invade England when he heard about the execution of Mary, Queen of Scots – the last straw.

Philip's plan

Note: Use the map on page 66.
1. Build the Armada – the Spanish word for invasion fleet.
2. Sail up the Channel, and join forces with Parma's army in the Netherlands.
3. Guard Parma's soldiers as they crossed the Channel in barges.
4. Land in England and take London. Make England Catholic.

Philip's beard is singed

By the spring of 1587 Philip's Armada was nearly ready in Cadiz harbour. Suddenly English warships led by Francis Drake sailed into the harbour and attacked the Spanish fleet. Drake said he destroyed 37 ships at Cadiz. A report sent to Philip said 24. Drake also burnt a lot of wood waiting to be made into storage barrels. When the Armada sailed a year later, many barrels leaked or split, because they were made of the wrong wood. Drake said cheekily afterwards he had singed the King of Spain's beard. But beards grow again. Philip rebuilt his ships.

Philip had other problems. So did Elizabeth.

The Spanish feared Francis Drake more than any other English sailor. They called him El Draque, *the dragon*. They thought he had a magic mirror which let him see over the horizon because he attacked so many treasure ships. Drake sailed round the world (1577–80), and returned with treasure worth £600 000. The Queen made him a knight. This tiny portrait of the weatherbeaten seaman was painted then.

In the summer of 1588, Philip's Armada was ready to sail. The Spanish Government published full details, which were printed and sold all over Europe, including England:

Ships Galleons, other fast fighting ships, supply ships: 130.

Men Sailors, soldiers, officers and their servants, gunners, doctors, 180 friars and priests: over 30 000.

Arms Cannons, and small guns: 1900. Cannon balls 123 790. Also powder, bullets, pikes, armour, swords.

Food and drink Biscuits, bacon, fish, cheese, rice, beans, wine, vinegar, water.

1 This sort of information about a fighting force would be Top Secret today. Why did the Spaniards publish it?

2 The English published it too, adding such things as whips, thumbscrews, racks, and pincers. Why did they do that?

Philip's problems
- There were no harbours in the Netherlands deep enough for the big Spanish ships. So picking up the Duke of Parma's army would be difficult. Philip ignored this problem.
- Parma's army needed a huge number of barges to get to England. He had to build them. And if the weather was rough, the barges might sink.
- It was very difficult to find all the supplies needed for the huge Armada.

Elizabeth's problems
- The Armada was a huge fleet, and a terrible threat.
- The English did not know about Philip's problems – nor what his plan was. The Armada might land anywhere.
- Supplies were difficult for the English fleet too.
- English land defences were weak. Most soldiers were untrained and badly equipped. Parma's army was the best in Europe. If he landed, he would be very difficult to defeat.

This picture, painted soon after 1588, gives an idea of English and Spanish fighting ships, though the artist probably did not see the battle. People thought the Spanish ships were bigger because they had high forecastles. They were designed to fight the enemy at close quarters, so they carried a lot of soldiers. Their cannons were not so effective.

In fact the biggest ship in the battle was English. But the English ships were faster and low in the water. They were better at firing at the enemy from some distance, and did not carry soldiers.

Diary of the Armada's journey ← 28

Late spring Departure delayed: sickness in the crew, shortage of supplies, bad weather. The English fleet in Plymouth harbour had the same problems.

20 May Armada set sail from Lisbon.

19 June Delays because of storms. Armada had to stop at Corunna for more supplies.

19 July The English saw the Armada off the coast of Cornwall. Beacons lit from hilltop to hilltop to warn everybody.

21 July English fleet led by Lord Howard, Drake and Sir John Hawkins, sailed out of Plymouth. A running fight up the Channel. But the English could not break the Spanish crescent.

27 July Spanish fleet anchored off Calais. They still did not know where to meet Parma, or if he knew they had arrived. The English sent in 'hellburners' – fireships which were very frightening, but in fact caused no damage. But the captains of the Spanish ships cut their anchors to escape – and the crescent was broken.

The next six days A desperate battle. English guns badly damaged the Spanish ships, but they fought on. Then the English ran out of ammunition. The battered Armada was still a threat, but the wind blew it steadily northwards. The Spanish could not go home the way they had come.

Meanwhile in England: 29 July The Queen and her councillors still thought the Spanish would invade. The Queen visited her troops at Tilbury, near London, and made a rousing speech:

> I ... am resolved in the midst and heat of battle to live and die amongst you all ... I know I have the body of a weak and feeble woman, but I have the heart and stomach of a king, and a King of England too, and think foul scorn that Parma, or Spain, or any prince of Europe should dare to invade the borders of my realm.

Everyone cheered. Everyone was ready to fight to the death. but Parma and his Spanish army never came.

The end of the story The Spanish had a terrible stormy journey home, right round the north of Scotland, and Ireland. Many ships were wrecked, mainly off the rocky coast of Ireland. The rest

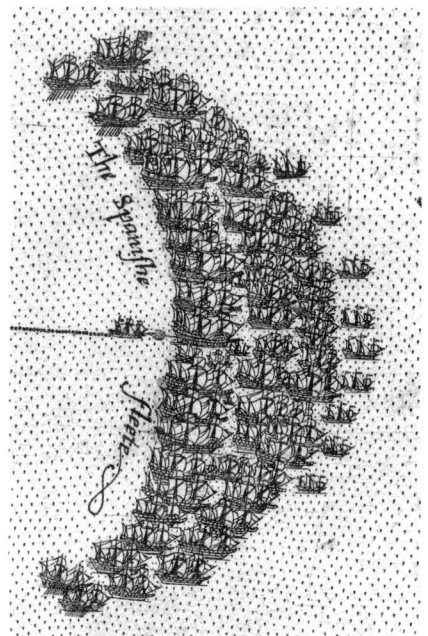

The Armada sailed in a strong crescent formation. The best warships sailed on the outer rim and on the horns. If there was an attack from behind, the horns closed in and protected the heavy supply ships in the centre. The Spanish had to be skilful sailors to keep this formation, whatever the weather. Until the crescent broke, the English could not attack the Armada successfully.

65

limped home during September and October to Santander, full of wounded, starving and sick men. About 44 ships were lost. The English fleet was not so badly damaged, and near home. But their ships were full of sick men too. They lay dying (probably of typhus) in the streets of English ports, and Elizabeth did not find enough money even to give them their pay. Admiral Lord Howard wrote sadly to the Queen's advisers:

> It would grieve any man's heart to see them that have served so valiantly to die so miserably.

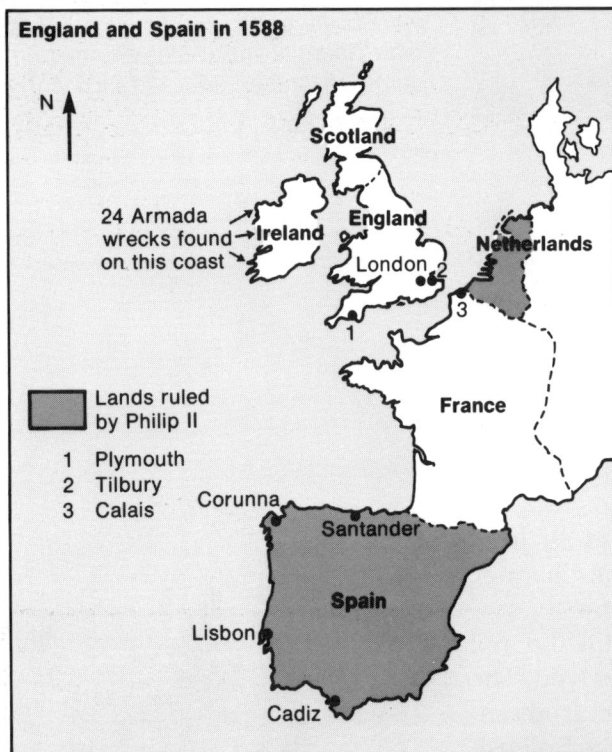

England and Spain in 1588

N

Scotland

24 Armada wrecks found on this coast → Ireland

England

London

Netherlands

France

Lands ruled by Philip II

1 Plymouth
2 Tilbury
3 Calais

Corunna

Santander

Spain

Lisbon

Cadiz

1 Make your own copy of this map. Show Philip's plan in one colour, and the actual route of the Armada in another.

2 Under the map, write your own version of the story of the Armada.

3 Each of the following had some part in the defeat of the Armada. Put what you think is the most important at the top, and arrange the rest in order underneath. Discuss the reasons for your order with the rest of the class:

- Weakness in Philip's plan ● Shortage of supplies ● No help for Spain from English Catholics ● The weather ● English guns and ships ● No modern communications system

4 Write an eye-witness account of the 'hell burners' at Calais, from the English or Spanish point of view. Use what you know about life on board ship ← 28 , and the events so far.

War leaders

The commander of the Armada, the Duke of Medina Sidonia, did not want the job. He wrote to Philip in February 1588:

> My health is not equal to such a voyage . . . I am always seasick, and always catch cold. My family is burdened with debt . . . Since I have no experience of the sea I cannot feel that I ought to command so important an enterprise.

We also know that Medina Sidonia did the best he could to organise supplies. He took advice from experienced seamen. His ship was always in the thick of the battle, even though he was often ill. Philip did not blame him for the defeat. The King said afterwards:

> I sent my ships to fight against men, and not against the winds and waves of God.

1 What are Medina Sidonia's reasons against being the commander of the Armada? Do you think he was a bad leader?

2 What is your opinion of Philip and Elizabeth as war leaders? (Pick out what each of them did in the story before you decide.)

A great victory?

The war dragged on, and Spain remained a danger to England. Of course the English thought the defeat of the Armada was a great victory. After all, the Spanish army had never landed. They were still free, Protestant and ruled by their English Queen. This picture was probably painted about 20 years later, and hangs in a small Lincolnshire church. It shows the Armada like an evil crescent-shaped red dragon. The English fireships attack it. At the top, Spanish ships are wrecked off Scotland and Ireland. At the bottom, English soldiers with the flag of St George are the winners.

The Armada had another result. English Catholics could have supported Catholic Spain – but they did not. There were no rebellions or plots in 1588, and they stayed loyal. But it did them no good. Most English people did not forget that the enemy had been Catholic. They thought Catholics were traitors ← 63, and could never be trusted. Catholics still had a very difficult time.

> ■ Why does the picture use the story of St George and the Dragon to show the fight between England and Spain? 1

Key words in this chapter to help you remember and understand what you have learnt. You should be able to use these words now, and find evidence in this chapter which illustrates each of them

Henry VIII
divorce
heir
Supreme Head of the Church
Archbishop
Chancellor
monastery
convent
investigation
lead roofs
treasure
land
English Bible

Edward VI
Protestant
council

Mary I
Catholic
marriage
persecution
heretic
martyr

Elizabeth I
cautious
Church of England

Mary, Queen of Scots
marriages
murder
rebellion
plots
traitor
execution

Armada
invasion
crescent
supplies
land defence
beacons
fireships
barges
storms
shipwreck
typhus
defeat
victory

5 Elizabethan people

This is one of the grandest portraits of Elizabeth I, painted to celebrate the Armada victory. Find in the picture: the battle raging in a stormy sea; the victorious English fleet, sailing in a calm sunny sea; the crown; the globe. The Queen's hand is on America – why? ← 64

1 Notice as much as you can about the Queen's costume. ◁3▷

2 How many things can you see in the portrait which show Elizabeth is a powerful and successful Queen? ◁1▷

This tiny painting, called a miniature, was not much bigger than a 10p coin. We are lucky to have it, because it shows the Queen as an old woman. Elizabeth did not employ this artist, Isaac Oliver, again. Are you surprised? How can you tell it is not finished?

1 How does the visitor show he thinks the Queen looks old? ◁1▷

2 Is he impressed by her? Explain your answer. ◁1▷

3 Which portrait on this page is most like this description? ◁1▷

4 Why did the Queen not want to look old in her portraits, and why did she take such trouble about them? ◁2▷

Elizabeth I and her courtiers

Queen Elizabeth I had strong views about her portraits. Early in her reign she made a proclamation that all portraits of her had to be from special 'face patterns' (rather like dress patterns) approved by her. These 'patterns' were copied many times, in portraits, on coins and on official seals for government documents. Ordinary people could buy cheap engravings (printed drawings) so they saw the 'patterns' too.

The Armada portrait uses one of these face patterns. When it was painted, Elizabeth was nearly 60. You already know what she looked like as a young woman. ← 58 In 1562 she almost died of smallpox. It can leave terrible scars. Perhaps Elizabeth was lucky, but as she got older she wore a lot of thick white make-up, and a red wig – she may have lost her hair when she was ill. Does she look her age in this picture?

This is how a foreign visitor described Elizabeth when he saw her in a grand procession in 1598, only a few years later:

> Next came the Queen, in the sixty-sixth year of her age ... very majestic: her face oblong, fair but wrinkled; her eyes small, yet black and pleasant; her nose a little hooked; her lips narrow, and her teeth black ... she had in her ears two pearls, with very rich drops; she wore false hair, and that red.

Fashion at Elizabeth's court

This drawing is based on the famous Ditchley Portrait of Queen Elizabeth in the National Portrait Gallery, which you can see on the first page of this book. It shows the Queen wearing one of her grandest dresses. Portraits tell us a lot about fashionable clothes worn by the rich people at Elizabeth's court. The portraits on pages 70 and 71 show what fashionable male courtiers wore.

Hairstyles Women wore their hair like the Queen's – frizzed out, and with jewelled ornaments.

Sleeves were padded with horsehair. They were separate from the dress, and had to be pinned or tied on with tapes. People sometimes gave 'a pair of sleeves' as a present.

Fans The Queen owned many fans of different designs. Here is a description of one from a list of the Queen's clothes of 1600:

One fan of white feathers, with a handle of gold, having two snakes winding about it, . . . with a ball of diamonds at the end . . . and a crown on each side within a pair of wings.

Stomacher A long V-shaped bodice, stiffened with whalebone or strips of wood. It made women look as if they had a tiny waist.

Farthingale A framework made of whalebone, which held out the layers of skirts. This shape is called a wheel farthingale.

Make-up Unlike today, no one wanted to look tanned. Elizabeth's white make-up was made from powdered eggshells, egg white, alum, borax and poppy seeds mixed with mill-water. Sometimes women used white lead to get the fashionable pale effect. This was dangerous and could cause skin cancer.

Ruffs You can see two shapes of these big lace collars on these pages and on the title page. But how did they stand up so stiffly? The answer was starch, which first came to England from Holland in 1564.

Materials Look at the Armada portrait as well as the title page. The Queen wore materials covered with jewels, and other decoration. Here is a description of one of her petticoats (the overskirt was split to show it at the front, like the Armada dress). It comes from the list of the Queen's clothes of 1600:

One petticoat of white satin, embroidered all over . . . with snakes of gold, silver, and silk of many colours, with a fair border, embroidered with seas, clouds, and rainbows.

1 Make your own labelled picture of this portrait of the Queen. Then make a classroom collage of Elizabethan fashion. Use the descriptions of the fan and petticoat too. ⊲1⊐ ⊲3⊐

2 Look carefully at these pictures and think what it must have been like to get dressed, and to wear clothes like this. How would you sit, stand and walk? ⊲2⊐

The marriage game

Elizabeth I was a woman in a world of men. And of course, everyone expected her to get married, just like her older sister Mary. ←55 Philip of Spain considered marrying her when she became Queen – to 'relieve her of those labours which are only fit for men', as he kindly said.

Elizabeth knew how much people disliked Mary's marriage. But she needed Philip as a friend at the beginning of her reign, and did not want to offend him. So she pretended she was interested for a time. Later other foreign princes suggested marriage. If Elizabeth wanted their country's friendship, she often seemed on the point of marrying – but she never actually did . . .

Robert Dudley, Earl of Leicester At the beginning of Elizabeth's reign, people thought she would marry the handsome Robert Dudley. He was her Master of Horse, and constantly by her side. She made him the Earl of Leicester. What sort of person does he look like? Many courtiers were very jealous of him.

But Leicester was married. Then his wife Amy was found dead at the bottom of a staircase in their home at Cumnor, near Oxford. She had been ill, lonely, and depressed, while her husband was at court. Some people thought she committed suicide. Or was she murdered? Most probably it was an accident, but it did Leicester no good.

The Queen sent him away from court for a time. He married twice more. Each time Elizabeth was furious. But she forgave him. In 1575 the whole court visited his castle at Kenilworth. There were all kinds of entertainments, and the clock on the castle tower was stopped, so that time stood still while the Queen was there.

When the Queen died, her ladies opened a little box she kept by her bedside. They found a letter Leicester had written just before he died in 1588. On it she had written 'His last letter'.

Did Elizabeth want to marry? Elizabeth sometimes seemed to want to marry, but we do not know what she really felt. Some things she said are clues.

To Members of Parliament, when they asked her to marry in 1566:

> I have already joined myself to a husband, namely the Kingdom of England . . . Though I be a woman, yet I have as good a courage as my father had. I am your anointed Queen . . . I thank God I am endowed with such qualities that [the kind of person who] if I were turned out of my realm in my petticoat, I were able to live in any place . . . I will marry as soon as I conveniently can.

To the Earl of Leicester when he ordered one of her servants about:

> I will have here but one mistress and no master.

The Earl of Leicester is dressed in the height of fashion. He wears a small velvet cap with a feather, and a high lace ruff. Why do you think Elizabethan men wore their hair short?
His doublet (jacket) is pink silk with tiny slits all over it which show gold embroidery underneath. Notice the V shape.
His trunk hose (short padded pants) are the same colour, and though you cannot see them, he wears tights and square-toed shoes.
A gentleman of high rank wore a sword, and you can see Leicester's coat of arms (family badge) as well. Everything in this portrait tells you how rich and important he is!

1 What were the disadvantages if Elizabeth married? ←55 ◁4▱

2 What were the disadvantages if Elizabeth did not marry? ←33 ◁4▱

3 Why do you think Elizabeth did not get married? ◁4▱

Sunshine and storms

Elizabeth's courtiers were fond of flattering the Queen by saying that when she smiled it was like the sun shining, and when she was angry it was like a terrible storm. She liked to be called the 'Fairy Queen' too, even when she was a middle-aged woman wearing a wig and a lot of make-up. She gave her favourites nicknames. Leicester was her 'Eyes'.

Her most trusted servant was William Cecil. She called him her 'Spirit'. When she became Queen she said to him:

> This judgement I have of you that . . . you will be faithful to the state, and that . . . you will give me that *counsel* [advice] which you think best.

The Queen was right about Cecil. He was sensible and practical, and served her faithfully till he died in 1598, almost at the end of her reign. During his last illness, the Queen sat with him and fed him herself.

Sir Walter Raleigh (the Queen nick-named him 'Water' after his name) was a poet, soldier and explorer. He is supposed to have laid his fine cloak over a puddle for the Queen to walk on, so her shoes would not get muddy. The story tells us how courtiers treated the Queen, even if it is not true.

Compare his ruff with Leicester's. This big wheel shape was fashionable later in Elizabeth's reign, so it helped experts to decide that this portrait was painted in about 1585.

A rude letter

Elizabeth could get very angry too. Once she wanted to give some land to her favourite, Sir Christopher Hatton. The land belonged to the Bishop of Ely. Not surprisingly, he refused to give it up. This is the letter Elizabeth wrote to him:

> Proud *Prelate* [bishop]:
> You know what you were before I made you what you are now. If you do not immediately comply with my request, I will *unfrock* [dismiss] you by God.

1 Write down as many reasons as you can why this letter is so rude.

2 This is the signature Elizabeth always used. Make your own 'old copy' of the letter and copy her signature as well as you can.

The Queen arriving at one of her grandest palaces, Nonsuch, near Kingston-on-Thames. She is travelling in an open coach. Coaches were very new in Elizabeth's reign, and made it easier for women to travel. The Queen was a good rider, but many women found their tight costumes and huge skirts made long journeys on horse-back difficult.

The Queen on her travels

In the summer, Elizabeth liked to go on a 'progress'. She visited important towns, and great houses belonging to her courtiers.

She enjoyed seeing different places, and she could learn about her subjects too. They could actually see their Queen. Also, she never liked spending money. When she and the court visited a nobleman's house, he paid the bills.

People who entertained the Queen and her court must have had mixed feelings. They were probably thrilled by the honour – and pleased at how impressed their neighbours would be. But the work and expense were huge. Sometimes a house owner decided he must alter his house to make it grander and bigger. About 200 people had to be fed. When the Queen's party visited Cowdray Park in Sussex, they ate three oxen and 140 geese just for breakfast, and that was before all the banquets started. There were entertainments too – plays, dances, hunts, picnics and firework displays. When the Queen stayed with the Earl of Leicester, the entertainments lasted three weeks.

The Queen loved it all. In 1600 some courtiers grumbled about going on a progress. The Queen (aged nearly 67) told them crossly that the old could stay behind, and the young and active come with her.

Elizabeth I loved active sports almost to the end of her life – especially hunting. What animal has she just killed? Her horse and hunting dogs are behind her. Her hunting costume, of course, was simpler than her grand court dresses.

Facts and figures

Four hundred carts and 2400 packhorses transported everyone's belongings. The Queen's procession travelled about ten miles a day. During her reign, she stayed at 241 different places. These are some of the places she visited (she never went beyond the ones on this list): Winchester, Southampton, Coventry, Oxford, Cambridge, Ipswich, Norwich, Harwich, Stamford, Bristol, Warwick, Kenilworth, Wilton, Longleat, Chichester, Cowdray Park.

This is an eye-witness description of a progress in 1568:

> She was received with great acclamations and signs of joy ... whereat she was extremely pleased ... She ordered her carriage sometimes to be taken where the crowd seemed thickest and stood up and thanked the people.

1 On an outline map of England, mark in the places the Queen visited. How far from London did she travel? Which areas did she never visit? Why do you think she never got there?

2 The Queen travelled little in the 1580s. Why not? (Clue ← 64–7)

3 How does the eye-witness account compare with a public appearance by Elizabeth II? Think of some differences.

4 How do we know so much about what the present Queen does? How much do you think ordinary people knew about Elizabeth I? (Clues Where did they live? What pictures might they have seen?)

5 Write a letter from a courtier to his wife at home. The Queen is coming to stay, and his wife must get everything ready.

Bess of Hardwick

Bess of Hardwick, Countess of Shrewsbury, was a woman who knew what she wanted. Many rich Elizabethan men built themselves grand new houses. Bess built more than most, and organised everything herself. Her most famous house is Hardwick

Hall in Derbyshire, built in the local sandstone. It is almost the same today as it was in Bess's time. Many of her possessions are still there. They are on an inventory (list) she made in 1601.

'Hardwick Hall, more glass than wall' had huge windows – a new fashion. They still had small diamond-shaped panes joined by lead strips, which came from Bess's own lead mines. Glass was cheaper now, but was only made in small pieces. There was also a fashionable Long Gallery stretching almost 52 metres along the top of the house. It was hung with tapestries and portraits, and used for all kinds of social occasions. The women of the house would walk there when the weather was too bad to go out.

Evidence on Hardwick

A

Bess was born a working farmer's daughter. She married first when she was 13. Her husband soon died, and left her land and lead mines in Derbyshire. She was a rich widow, and a good catch. That put her on the ladder to the top (see below). When she died at the great age of 87, she was Countess of Shrewsbury, and her grand-daughter had royal blood from her father's family. You can get a good idea of the kind of person she was from the events of her life, and the way she organised the building of Hardwick.

B Three items from Bess's accounts:

'Paid to John Roads for hewing of two windows . . . for [each of] the turrets, forty eight shillings.' He also got 3d a foot (0.3048 m) for the carving at the top of the turrets.

Abraham Smith made the decorated plaster ceilings. He was paid £3 6s 8d for 3 months work, and 40s as a wedding present.

A 'cradle' for the glazier cost 8d. ← 2

1 Look carefully at **A**. How did Bess (Elizabeth Shrewsbury) make sure everyone knew who had built Hardwick when they looked at the outside of the house? 1

2 How many windows are there on the side of the house you can see? (Be careful!) Which windows face out from the Long Gallery? Are they different from the others? If so, why? Which windows did John Roads 'hew'? 1

3 Look up glazier in the dictionary. How was the 'cradle' used? 4

4 How can you tell that:
a) Bess was a good business woman?
b) she knew her workmen well? 1

5 How much primary evidence can you find on this page? 1

> **Bess's rise to the top**
> *1533, aged 13* First marriage to Robert Barlow.
> *1547, aged 27* Second marriage to Sir William Cavendish, a rich landowner. Six children born. Cavendish died 10 years later.
> *1559, aged 39* marriage to Sir William St Loe. Bess went to court. St Loe died five years later.
> *1568, aged 48* the last and grandest marriage to the Earl of Shrewsbury. The couple had to guard Mary Queen of Scots. This led to trouble, and terrible quarrels. In the end they separated.
> *1590, aged 70* Death of the Earl of Shrewsbury. Bess began to build Hardwick.
> *1597, aged 77* Hardwick finished. Bess went to live there.
> *1607, aged 87* Bess died.

Members of Parliament

Queen Elizabeth I is sitting on a throne in Parliament. She is in the House of Lords. Her important councillors stand round her.

The other members of the **House of Lords** are in the middle of the picture – they are noblemen, judges, and bishops.

Members of Parliament (MPs) have come in from the **House of Commons** to attend the Queen. They are in the front of the picture. They are rich people too – mainly country gentlemen. They want to be sure the Queen understands how they feel about important matters, such as her marriage, religion and money.

The Speaker stands in the middle and is making a speech to the Queen. He is the most important person in the House of Commons, and the Queen's trusted servant. He decides what shall be discussed, who shall speak and for how long. He knows the Queen does not like MPs to discuss some things without her permission, such as her marriage, religion and money.

Parliament became more important in Tudor times, mainly because Henry VIII used it to make himself Head of the Church. But it was very different from the modern British Parliament. This diagram shows how:

1 Who was the most powerful in Elizabeth I's time – Parliament, the council or the Queen? Arrange in order, most powerful at the top.

2 Now arrange the order of power in modern Britain – the Queen, Parliament, government, voters. You will need to discuss it!

3 Elizabeth was short of money, especially at the end of her reign. Find a reason why this meant she needed to be tactful, and sometimes gave in to her Parliaments (though it was never over her marriage or religion).

4 The present Queen only goes to Parliament for the opening ceremony once a year. Find out what happens. Who writes the speech she makes?

Elizabeth I		Elizabeth II
Men who owned or rented land had the vote. They almost always voted for the most important people in their area.	**The vote**	All British men and women over 18 have the vote, except members of the House of Lords and prisoners.
Held when the Queen decided	**Elections**	Must be held every five years.
Rich men. Almost all MPs were land-owners. They were not paid, so they had to be rich.	**Members of Parliament**	Any British man or woman can be an MP. They are paid, so it does not matter whether they are rich or poor.
The Queen and her council	**The Government**	The Government is chosen from the party which has the most MPs in the House of Commons.
Elizabeth I told Parliament what laws she wanted them to pass. They usually agreed.	**The Queen's power** **Making laws**	Elizabeth II has no power over Parliament. The Government decides what laws Parliament must pass.
She told Parliament when she needed more money. They did not always grant all she needed.	**Money**	The Government decides how money from everyone's taxes should be spent.

Londoners

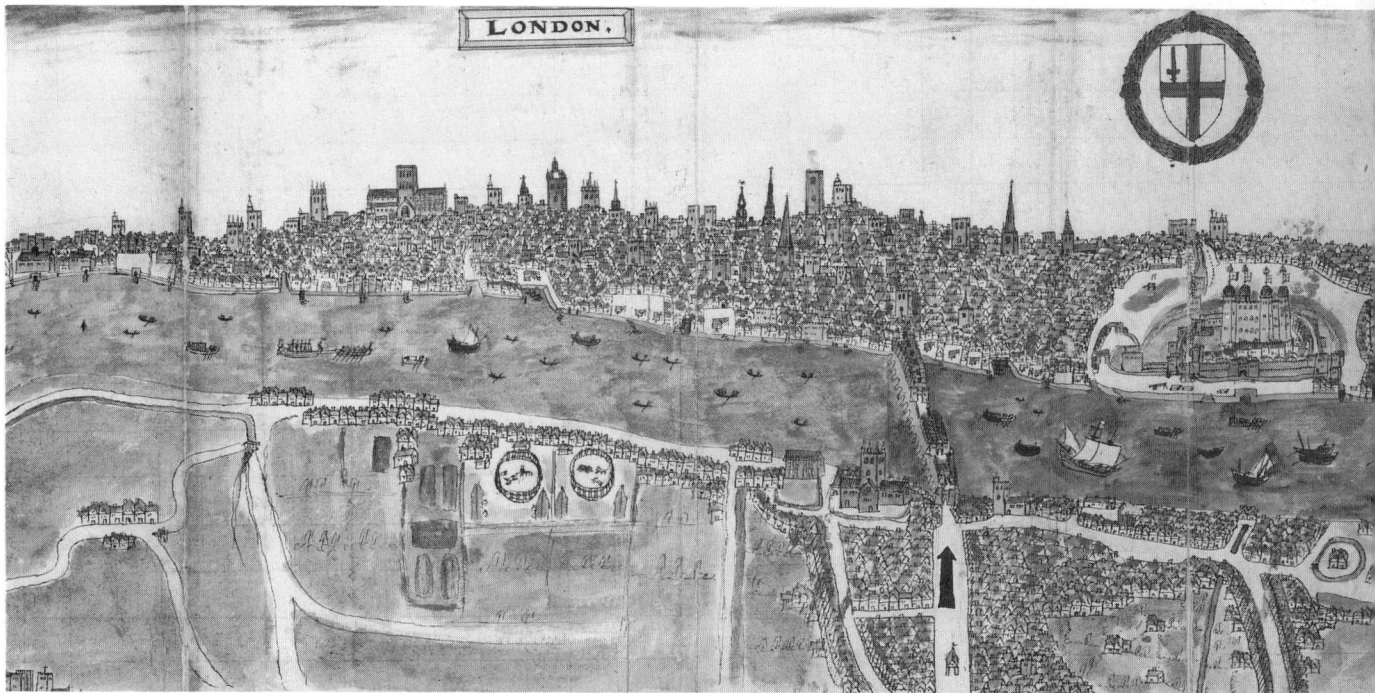

Imagine you can walk into this picture of Elizabethan London. You are a country person, on your first visit. You arrive from the south, on the road where the big arrow is. So the first thing you do is to cross the River Thames by London Bridge. This is the only bridge in London, and you have never seen a bridge like it before, with shops, houses and a church on it. It has narrow arches. At high tide when the river flows fast, London apprentices enjoy shooting through them in small boats. On the gateway are rotting traitors' heads – to remind everyone what happens to people caught plotting against the Queen.

The river is really one of London's most important roads. It is much pleasanter to travel by river than along dirty, crowded streets. Above the bridge you can see the big merchant ships unloading cargoes of silks, spices, leather hides, iron and coal. There are many 'strangers' (foreigners) speaking languages you do not understand. Watermen's boats are everywhere. These are like taxis, and you can hire one if you want. You may be lucky and see the Queen's barge pass by. It is decorated with cloth of gold and crimson velvet, and musicians play to her and her courtiers.

The city is crammed with buildings, from grand goldsmiths' shops in the main shopping street, Cheapside, to tumbledown hovels in tiny back alleys. The most famous building is St Paul's, the biggest church on the skyline, with a square tower. Its tall pointed steeple was struck by lighting in 1561, so you must be visiting London after that date.

■ Write an illustrated story about your first day in Elizabethan London. Use the information on page 76 and 77, and find out more if you can.

THE CITY OF LONDON

ⵊⵊⵊ Walls

■ Gates
(Modern street names still tell us where these are.)

To the north and north-west

CRIPPLEGATE

MOORGATE

To York and the north-east

ALDERSGATE

River Fleet

To the west

NEWGATE

BISHOPSGATE

To the east

Cheapside

LUDGATE

ALDGATE

St Paul's Church

Fleet Street

The Strand

River Thames

THE TOWER

Bull baiting ○

Bear baiting ○

LONDON BRIDGE

Globe ○

To the Thames estuary and the sea

PALACE OF WHITEHALL

THE CITY OF WESTMINSTER

Abbey

Parliament

To the south

The Long Ditch

LAMBETH PALACE

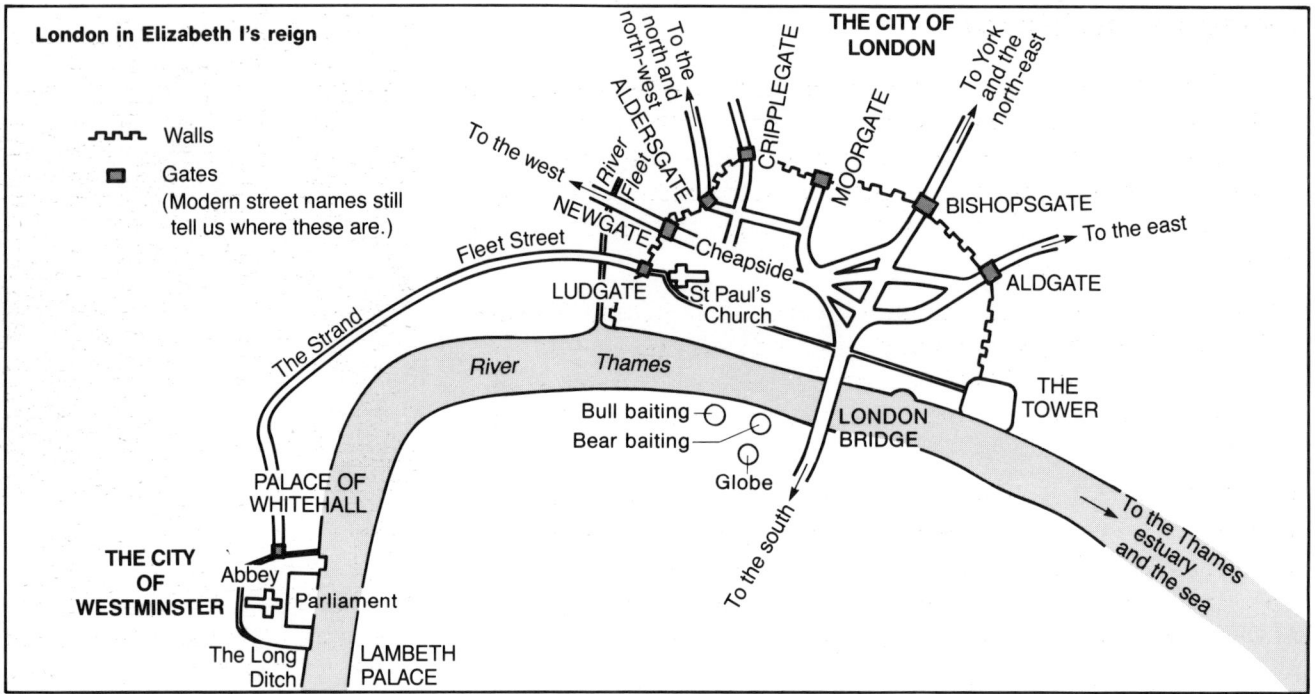

People in the streets

Paremptitius

The water carrier fills his 12-litre wooden container from a water pump in the street. The water comes from the river in wooden pipes. (And most of the city's rubbish as well as the few drains go into the river.) Only very big houses had water indoors, and no one had modern taps and toilets. Most people bought their water from the water carrier. How many reasons can you find for London water being very unhealthy?

The ballad seller has cheap news-sheets and ballads for sale – short, often amusing little rhymes which poke fun at people, or tell of some great event. Women and men work as ballad sellers. They sell other things too – ribbons, pins, buttons and so on. They travel round the country as well as London. They are the people who spread the news. There are no newspapers.

Beggars are everywhere in London streets. This picture comes from a pamphlet warning people there are many different kinds of beggars who might swindle them. Here are two of them. The 'Upright Man' (on the left) pretends he is a fine gentleman down on his luck. The 'Counterfeit Crank' (a false crooked character) pretends he is physically handicapped, and sometimes eats soap so that he froths at the mouth. But does this kind of picture mean that all beggars are like this?

The night watchman is supposed to walk the streets after dark at regular intervals, calling out the time and what the weather is like. (Sometimes he is lazy and dozes in a sheltered corner.) There are no policemen in Tudor England, so his job can be dangerous. The streets are dark unless householders put lanterns outside their doors – so he needs to carry his own light. What else in the picture helps him with his job?

Going to the theatre

If Londoners wanted to enjoy themselves, they often went south of the river. You can see two entertainments on the river bank in the picture opposite – the bull- and bear-baiting pits. Dogs were set on bulls and bears, and people bet on the result of the fight. This seems cruel to us now – why do we have a different attitude today?

There was a new entertainment nearby – the Globe Theatre, finished in 1599. You will not find it in the picture (so that shows it was painted earlier). Plays had been performed in streets and market squares before. Going to the theatre was new, exciting and fashionable.

The Globe was even more exciting because a young actor called William Shakespeare was writing most of the plays performed there. Rich and poor Londoners laughed at his comics, sympathised with the heroes and heroines, and wept at the tragedies. Audiences were much noisier than they are now.

You can see what the Globe was like from the two pictures in the margin. It was open to the sky. The stage jutted out into the pit – the ground level where poorer people could afford to go. They stood all through the performance, and got wet if it rained. The expensive seats were in the covered galleries round the edge. The most fashionable members of the audience often sat on the stage, or in the gallery behind the actors – where they could be seen along with the play! The two doors at the back of the stage led to the actors' dressing rooms. Stage equipment was kept there too.

Women enjoyed theatre going as well as men (Look at the people getting a free view outside the Globe in the top picture.) But women did not act. Boys played the female parts. Elizabeth I enjoyed plays too, but she did not go to the Globe. The actors went to the court, and the plays were often written especially to please her.

The outside of the Globe Theatre with the flag flying to show a performance was on. A trumpet announced the beginning of a play. The picture is from a map drawn in about 1600.

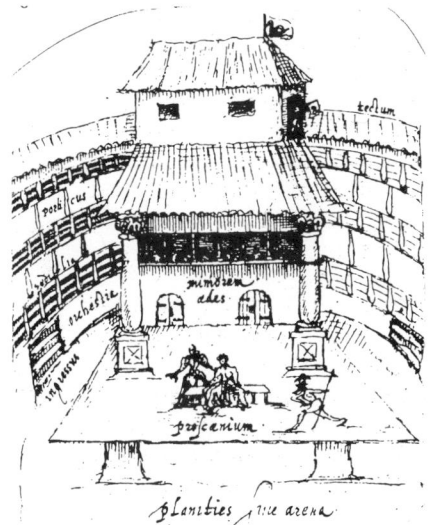

1. Draw a plan of the Globe Theatre, using both pictures to help you. Label clearly: the cheap and expensive seats, the stage, the gallery behind it, the entrance for the actors, the entrance to the pit, the place for the orchestra, the flag that shows the play is in progress. 3

2. Why were the people in the pit called 'groundlings'? 4

3. Describe a visit to the Globe. If you know a scene from Shakespeare's plays, you could make that the play you watch. Are you going to sit in the best seats, or be a groundling? 2

The Swan Theatre was built a few years after the Globe, and was very like it. This sketch was drawn at the time, and is our best evidence of what both theatres looked like inside.

Poor people

In 1570 the prosperous businessmen who ran the city of Norwich were worried. There were so many poor people in the city, and their numbers seemed to be growing. They were sorry for the poor and wanted to help them. But they also did not want other poor people, who did not live in Norwich, flocking in to the city to take advantage of any help they gave.

So they decided to make a census. This was a list of all the poor who lived in Norwich and 'dwelt here ever'. It gave a lot of information about them. It also said what the city was doing to help them – if anything. City officials could give alms (money or food), or send people to live in the 'church house' where they were given food and shelter. Here are three families in that census of 1570:

> Ann Buckle of the age of 40 years, widow . . . hath two children, the one of the age of 9 years and the other of 5 years that work lace, and hath dwelt here ever. No alms, but very poor.

> John Burr of the age of 54 years, *glazier* [puts glass in windows], very sick and work not, and Alice his wife . . . 40 years that spin, and have 7 *children*, [aged 20, 12, 10, 8, 6, 4, and 2 who] spin wool and have dwelt here ever – in his own house, no alms, *indifferent* [not quite so poor as the others].

> John Findley, of the age of 82 years, *cooper* [barrel maker] not in work, and Joan his wife, sickly that spin and knit, and have dwelt here ever – in the church house, very poor.

1 What questions did the city officials ask these families?

2 Find reasons in each case why these families were poor.

3 Why was John Burr slightly better off? What might still make it very difficult for this family to keep going?

4 Make a list of the children and their ages, and how they earn money. (Notice none of them go to school.)

5 In groups, bring one of these families to life, and act what happens when three important citizens come to get information for the census.

'Sturdy rogues'

Here is some evidence on rich people's attitudes to poor people who they thought were 'sturdy' – healthy, able to work, but unemployed. Many of these people wandered from place to place, looking for work. Better off people did not think much of them. Why did they have no jobs? They must be lazy – or drink too much. Didn't they really just want to beg, steal, and cause trouble?

B An Act of Parliament of 1531 said vagabonds and idle persons should be taken to the market place

> and there to be tied to the end of a cart naked and be beaten with whips . . . till his body be bloody . . . and after such punishment . . . shall return without delay . . . to the place where he was born . . . and there put himself to labour like as a true man ought to do.

C A report of a magistrate in Somerset sent to Elizabeth's council in 1596:

> And I may justly say that the infinite numbers of idle wandering people are the chiefest cause of the *dearth* [famine] . . . for they lie idly in the alehouses day and night, eating and drinking excessively.

A

A drawing made at the time showing what people thought a wandering family was like. (Look back at the picture of London beggars on page 76 as well.)

1 How do **A** and **B** show that nobody wanted wandering people in their neighbourhood? ⟨1⟩

2 Look at 'Hard times in the 1590s'. Do you think the magistrate in Somerset is right about the reason for the famine? Explain your answer, and why he thinks like this. ⟨2⟩ ⟨4⟩

3 How can you tell that the artist in **C** does not want you to be sorry for the family in his picture? (For instance, does the man really need a crutch?) ⟨1⟩

In Tudor England, richer people tried to do something about people who were too poor to live, even if they were not always sympathetic. In 1601, Elizabeth's Parliament passed a 'Poor Law', which tried to deal with both kinds of poor people.

Hard times in the 1590s
- The war with Spain dragged on
- Prices rose
- Wages did not
- There were not enough jobs
- Ex-soldiers and sailors joined the people looking for jobs
- Cold wet summers meant several bad harvests one after the other
- In 1596 and 1597, there was famine amongst the poor

The Poor Law of 1601

The old, the sick and young children who were too poor to live were to be given alms, or shelter in the local 'poor house', if local officials thought they deserved it.

The poor who were healthy and energetic were to be given materials to work with – such as wool, hemp or flax.

Money to pay for both kinds of help was collected from a local tax called a 'rate'.

Anyone who refused to work had to go to prison.

This law lasted for over 200 years. It worked quite well if local people were generous. It certainly did not cure poverty, but it was a beginning.

1 In your acting group, bring to life a scene when the family in **C** come into Norwich, and meet the three city officials in one of the main streets. ⟨2⟩

2 What are attitudes like now to travelling people? ⟨4⟩

3 Discuss in class how this Poor Law compares with the help given to poor people now. ⟨4⟩

4 Why are some people poor, and others not? ⟨4⟩

Key words in this section to help you remember and understand what you have learnt. You should be able to use these words now and find evidence in the chapter which illustrates them.

Elizabeth and her courtiers
portrait
miniature
make-up
ruff
stomacher
farthingale
doublet
trunk hose
marriage
flattery
favourite
progress
procession
packhorse

Bess of Hardwick
windows
lead
diamond panes
long gallery
mason
glazier
plasterer

Members of Parliament
House of Lords
House of Commons
Speaker
vote
election
government
Acts of Parliament
laws
taxes

London
River Thames
London Bridge
St Paul's Cathedral
Cheapside
The Globe Theatre
bull-baiting
bear-baiting

The poor
census
alms
church house*
rogues
beggars
unemployment
Poor Law
vagabonds

*often called the poorhouse or the workhouse

6 Unpopular kings

This grand portrait of James was painted towards the end of his life by a Dutch artist, Daniel Mytens. It may be rather flattering.

James I

In the cold spring of 1603, Queen Elizabeth became very ill. She sat on cushions on the floor for days, doing nothing. She refused to eat or take any medicine. In the end her servants carried her to bed. She had never said who should rule after her. Just before she died, she mumbled the name of James VI of Scotland, the son of Mary, Queen of Scots. ← 55

When James VI of Scotland rode south to become James I of England, people were excited to have a king again. There had been a lot of problems at the end of Elizabeth's reign. ← 79 So the old Queen was not as popular as she had been. Now they hoped a king would make things go better. And this king was married, with two sons and a daughter, so there were no more worries about who would rule next.

James I was very different from Elizabeth. He did not bother to be dignified. He wore padded clothes, because he was afraid of being stabbed, and this made him look fat. He dribbled, rolled his eyes a lot and walked in an odd kind of shuffle. He was rather lazy, and often went hunting when he should have been working. He spent too much money, especially on his favourites. Like all rulers then, James believed his power came from God (this was called 'the divine right of kings'). He was not very tactful about it, and was fond of giving Parliament lectures on how they must obey him.

James had good points too. He was clever, and had made a good job of ruling Scotland. He wanted peace, and stopped the expensive war with Spain that had dragged on since the Armada. He wanted to be fair to Catholics and Puritans. ← 59 As he ruled England and Scotland, he thought it would be sensible if they became one kingdom. (But the English and the Scots did not agree with him.) He also wrote a book against the new habit of smoking, saying it produced an 'oily kind of soot ... dangerous to the lungs'.

■ Make a list in two columns of James' good and bad points. Put stars by the ones which you think might make him unpopular with the English. (You may find you have to put stars on some of the good points.)

The Gunpowder Plot

Some of the people in the story. This Dutch picture shows the plotters in the Gunpowder Plot. The artist probably never saw any of them, but he has put their names – including Guy Fawkes, a Yorkshire soldier. Who is missing?

Robert Cecil was James's chief minister. He wanted to be sure the strict laws against Catholics were still carried out. The Gunpowder Plot was useful to him, because it frightened James, so the King did not make things easier for Catholics.

English Catholics were disappointed when James did nothing for them. Most of them just wanted to be able to have Catholic services. But in 1605, a small group made a desperate plot. The Gunpowder Plot is very famous – but there are some odd things about it, which have never been solved.

The plan To blow up the Houses of Parliament with gunpowder when the King came to open it. To kidnap the royal children and take over the government.

Stage 1 The plotters rented a house near the Houses of Parliament and began to dig a tunnel into a cellar right under them. But they came up against a wall three feet thick. They gave up, and found they could rent the cellar.

> No one has ever found any trace of this tunnel.

Stage 2 The plotters put 36 barrels of gunpowder in the cellar, hidden under piles of firewood.

> People could only buy gunpowder with a government licence. Would a licence be given to Catholics? And how did they get all those barrels into the cellar without anyone seeing?

Stage 3 One of the plotters, Thomas Tresham, decided to warn his brother-in-law Lord Monteagle. This is part of the letter Tresham wrote:

yet i saye they shall receyue a terrible blowe this parleament and yet they shall not seie who hurts them

(you can pick out this important sentence if you remember that s often looks like an f, and the spelling is odd):

> yet I saye they shall receyve a terrible blowe this parleament and yet they shall not seie who hurts them

> Lord Monteagle seemed to know straight away that this meant that when the King opened Parliament on 5 November, there would be a terrible explosion which would blow everyone sky high. He went straight to Cecil, who told the King.

Stage 4 Guy Fawkes was in the cellar on the night of 4 November, waiting to set light to the gunpowder. Guards searched the cellar and found him. He was taken to the Tower and tortured. After four days he told the whole story.

Stage 5 Soldiers arrested the other plotters. Some were shot – the two leaders, Catesby and Percy, with the same bullet. The others were brought to London. With Guy Fawkes, they were hanged, drawn and quartered in January 1606. Tresham was put in the Tower and died there in December 1605, no one knows how.

1 Write a paragraph or two explaining the Gunpowder Plot, and what you think happened. Look up the word 'treason', and write its meaning at the end.

2 Why did 5 November become a day of celebration every year? Discuss in class whether you think it still should be now.

Puritans and Pilgrims

Puritans were English Protestants who wanted to 'purify' the Church of England. They thought it was still much too like the Catholic Church. They hated and feared Catholics. ← 33, 59

Some Puritans lived very simply and strictly, and wore plain dark clothes. They disapproved of the theatre, cardgames and many country sports, especially if they were played on Sundays. These Puritans were often shopkeepers, or craftsmen like carpenters or weavers, who usually lived simply anyway. However, some Puritans were rich people who wore fashionable clothes and enjoyed some luxuries. You could not always tell a Puritan man or woman by what they wore.

Puritans got their nickname in Elizabeth's reign. The Queen refused to listen to them, because she did not want any more changes in the Church of England. They hoped James I might accept the changes they wanted. The King held a meeting at Hampton Court in 1604, but nothing came of it. Some Puritans were so disappointed that they decided to leave England.

The Pilgrim Fathers

This modern drawing shows what it must have been like on board the *Mayflower*. The ship was about 27 metres long and 8 metres wide. People had to bring everything they needed for their new life, including food which they had to cook themselves. The journey of 67 days was very stormy; the ship leaked; and many people became ill. A baby was born, and was called Oceanus.

The Pilgrim Fathers were a group of Puritans who decided to make a long and adventurous journey – to North America. They wanted to make a new life and a new church there. In 1620 they set sail from Plymouth in a small ship called the *Mayflower*. One hundred and two people crowded on board – too many, because they had planned to use two ships, but the second one was damaged. They were not all Puritans. Some people went to make their fortunes. Maybe some of the Puritans hoped to do that as well.

The Pilgrim Fathers came to a land they did not know. (It was soon called New England.) They had hoped to arrive further south in Virginia, where it was warmer. It was November, and they faced the worst of the winter. They had no shelter, and only the tools and food they brought with them. They were exhausted by the journey, and many of them were ill. They were also worried about the dangers lurking in the forests near the shore, especially Indians.

William Bradford soon became their leader. He kept a diary. These are some entries from it:

A   The first winter

That which was most sad . . . was that in two or three months' time, half of their company died, especially in January and February, being in the depth of winter, and wanting houses and other comforts, being infected with scurvy and other diseases . . . Sometimes there died two or three a day . . . scarce fifty remained. And of these there was but six or seven sound persons who . . . fetched them wood, made them fires, *dressed* [cooked] them meat, made them beds, washed their loathsome clothes . . . all this willingly and cheerfully . . . showing therein their true love unto their friends.

B   The Indians ← 26

All this while the Indians came skulking about them . . . but when any approached near them they would run away; and once they stole their [the Pilgrims'] tools where they had been at work and were gone to dinner.

But about 16 March, a certain Indian came boldly amongst them and spoke to them in broken English which they could well understand but marvelled at it . . . He was not of these parts but belonged to the eastern parts where some English ships came to fish. His name was Samoset. He told them also of another Indian whose name was Squanto . . . who had been in England and could speak better English than himself. They made peace with Squanto which hath now continued this 24 years. Squanto directed them how to *set* [sow] their corn, where to take fish, and other things.

C   Behaviour

Bradford found some newcomers playing games in the street, . . . some at stool ball and such like sports. So he went to them and took away their implements and told them it was against his conscience that they should play and others work. There should be no gaming or revelling in the streets. Since that time nothing hath been attempted, at least openly.

1 From the information about the Mullins family, make a family tree. (There is one on page 55 which will help you to see how to do it.) Put the servant by the side of it. Discuss with your teacher how you will show the people whose names Bradford does not give. Put a date for deaths when you can.

2 Write down as many facts as you can find in **F**. How long after the arrival of the *Mayflower* is Bradford writing? How do you know?

William Bradford made a list of the people on the Mayflower. Here is one family called Mullins. He does not always spell it the same way! Read it in pairs. It is not too difficult. Remember s often looks like an f:

D

> mr William Mullines, and his wife; and ·2· Children Joseph, & priscila; and a servant Robart Carter.

Later Bradford made a list showing what happened to each family. Here is what he wrote about the Mullins family:

E

> mr Mullines, and his wife, his sone, & his servant dyed the first winter. only his dougter priscila survived, and maried with John Alden, who are both living, and haue ·11· Children. And their eldest daughter is maried & hath fiue Children. See N.E. Memorial.

At the end of his two lists, Bradford wrote this:

F

> of these 100 persons which came first over, in this first ship together the greater halfe dyed in the generall mortality; and most of them in ·2· or three monthes time. And for those which survied though some were ancient & past procreation; & others left y placo and cuntrio; yet those few remaining are sprung up aboue ·160· persons, in this 30 years. And are now living in this presente year ·1650· besids many of their children which are dead, and come not within this account. And of the old stock (of one, & other) ther are yet living this present year ·1650· nere ·30· persons. Let the Lord haue y praise; who is the High preserver of men.

To help you – line 4 *mortality*: death lines 6–7 *some were ancient and past procreation*: some were too old to have children

Thanksgiving

William Bradford has told us that about 50 pilgrims survived that first terrible winter. He also tells us that many of them lived to be quite old, so they must have been tough.

In November 1621, when the pilgrims had been in New England for a year, they held a Thanksgiving Feast. They ate the local food of course – including wild turkeys, cranberries, and pumpkins. Ninety Indians joined in, and brought five deer to roast. Americans still celebrate Thanksgiving every November.

More settlers arrived. Life was still hard. Food was often short. Trouble grew between the settlers and the Indians. Not all the newcomers wanted to live as strict Puritans. But New England became part of the modern American nation. Americans are proud of the people who came on the *Mayflower*, and called them the Pilgrim Fathers.

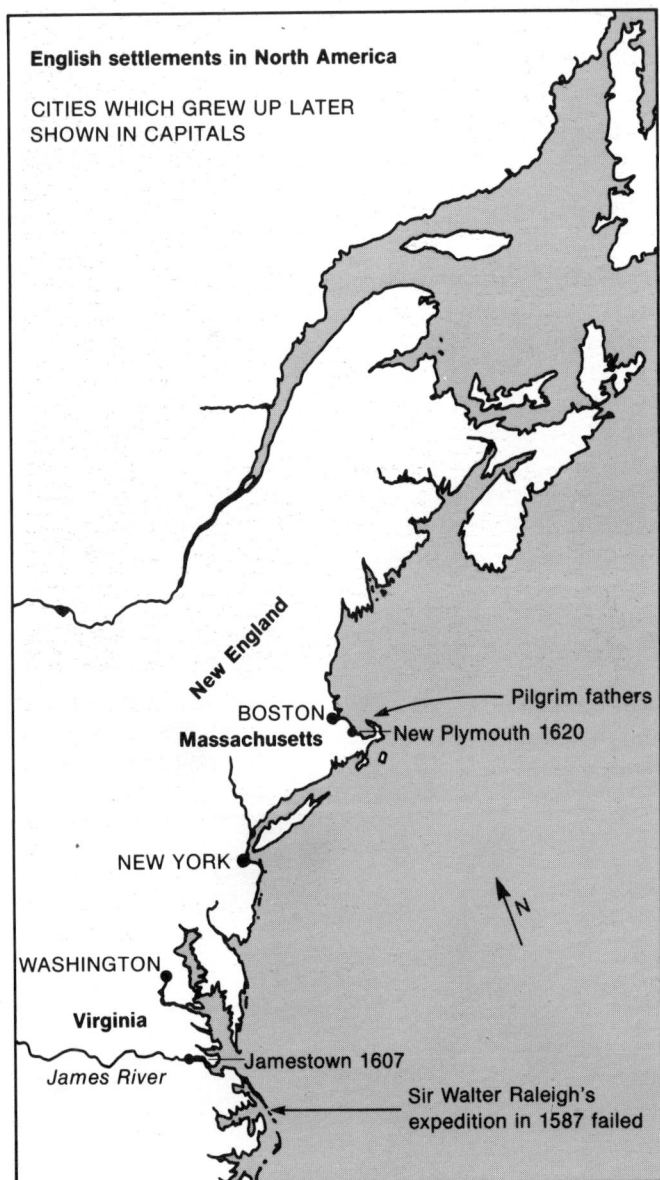

English settlements in North America

CITIES WHICH GREW UP LATER
SHOWN IN CAPITALS

New England

— Pilgrim fathers
BOSTON
Massachusetts New Plymouth 1620

NEW YORK

WASHINGTON

Virginia

Jamestown 1607
James River

Sir Walter Raleigh's
expedition in 1587 failed

1 Make a list of the difficulties the Pilgrims faced when they first landed. Use pages 82 and 83. There were 66 men, 26 women and 12 children. Think what everyone needed.

2 Why did the Pilgrims call the native Americans they met after they landed 'Indians'? ← 26 Read source **B** on page 83. What do you think the Pilgrims expected the Indians to be like, before they met Samoset and Squanto? How did Squanto help?

3 What evidence on page 83 tells you that Bradford and many of the Pilgrims were strict Puritans?

4 The place where the pilgrims settled became the colony of Massachusetts. Look up the word 'colony' and add its meaning to your fact list (page 83, question 2).

5 In a group of about six people, act or tape these two scenes:
a) November 1620. On board the *Mayflower* just after she has reached the coast of New England. Use your list (question 1), and work out what you must do to get through the winter.
b) April 1621. You are the lucky ones who have survived. The *Mayflower* sails back to England tomorrow. Work out the reasons why you might go back – and why you decide to stay.

6 Write some entries in a diary kept by Priscilla Mullins in 1620–1. She was about 20. Include: on board ship; the arrival; the death of her family; the spring comes – meeting Samoset; John Alden (a carpenter) asks her to marry him at Thanksgiving.

Charles I

Charles I became king in 1625. He was a very different character from his father. He was dignified and rather shy. He was artistic, and collected many beautiful pictures. He was very religious, and devoted to the Church of England.

He was also very bad at understanding how his subjects were feeling. He did not think it mattered anyway. He believed in the divine right of kings. ← 80 As his power came from God, he did not have to ask anybody's advice unless he felt like it.

His marriage made matters worse. His wife was a lively, elegant French princess, Henrietta Maria. Charles was devoted to her. She was Catholic, and you know what most English people felt about Catholics by now. She never really understood her new country, and she was always urging Charles on to be a strong King. She soon became very unpopular.

Charles I wanted his artists to show him as a great and powerful king. He employed Anthony Van Dyck, one of the best artists in Europe. How has the artist made us forget that Charles was a short man? (He was about 5 feet tall.) This picture is bigger than life size. It was probably hung at the end of a long corridor in Whitehall Palace, so that every one could see it from a long way away.

85

James I had trouble with Parliament. MPs wanted to have more say in running the country. There were quarrels over religion (many MPs were Puritans) and over money. James spent too much, and Parliament kept him short, because they did not always like the way he ruled. He began to find ways of raising money without asking Parliament. He increased customs duties, and sold people titles. Parliament grumbled about this, but nothing really serious happened while James was King.

Charles also spent too much money, on things like his great art collection. Parliament trusted him even less than James, and kept him short as well. But Charles was obstinate, and had no intention of sharing any of his power with Parliament, or of listening to MPs' advice.

So in 1629 Charles decided to rule without Parliament. But now he had to find enough money without asking Members of Parliament to vote him taxes. He found several different ways to do this. For instance, he raised customs duties again (this made things more expensive), and he made rich people pay to become knights. All this was unpopular, but most trouble came from a new tax.

Ship money

Charles wanted to build more ships for the navy. The King had the right to tax some ports to pay for new ships. In 1635, he made the whole country pay 'ship money'. Most people thought this was just another way of raising money without asking Parliament.

John Hampden was a rich Puritan landowner who lived in Buckinghamshire. He was not at all the kind of person to break the law. He had to pay £1 11s 6d in ship money. He could easily afford it, but he decided to refuse to pay – to show that he thought the King was wrong. He was tried before 12 of the King's judges in London. Seven of the judges found him guilty – probably to please the King – but nothing more happened. Most people thought Hampden had won.

However, for the moment, Charles had just enough money, as long as he did not spend anything extra – for instance on a war.

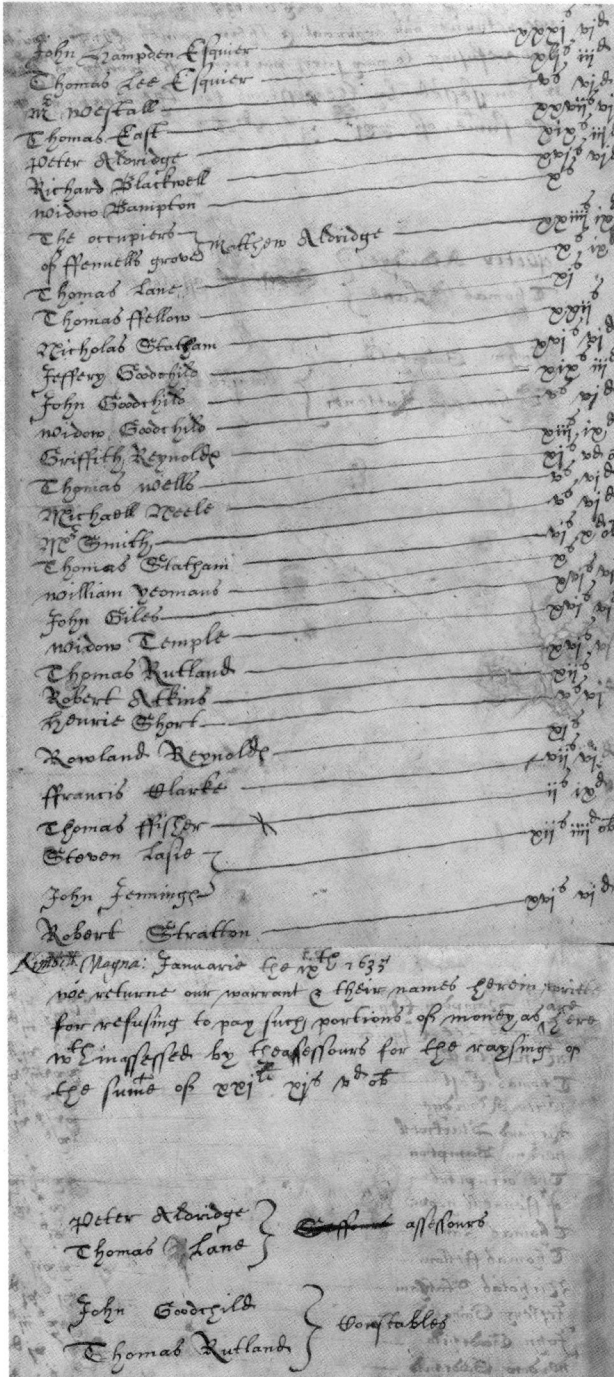

This is a page from the parish book from Great Kimble, Buckinghamshire, where John Hampden lived. It shows a list made at a meeting of about 31 local people held on 9 January 1635. They all refused to pay ship money. John Hampden's name is at the top. There are quite a lot of people who were not rich and did not have to pay so much. Find Mrs Westall (paid 5s 6d), Widow Bampton (paid 10s), and Thomas Lane (paid 10s 9d) ← 2 . What does this list show about the kind of people who refused to pay ship money in this village?

Trouble about religion

An unpopular archbishop   Charles I's Archbishop of Canterbury was called William Laud. He was a hard-working and sincere man, but he was also tactless and fussy – the kind of person who easily upset other people. The King and Archbishop both disliked Puritans, and thought they caused trouble. They wanted Church of England services to be more dignified, with beautiful music, candles on the altar, and more statues and pictures in church. Laud also made rules to stop Puritan sermons.

1 Why did Laud's ideas upset Puritans? ← 82

2 What else about Charles upset them? ← 85

Trouble in Scotland   Charles I was King of Scotland too ← 80 . In 1637, he ordered the Scots to use the Church of England Prayer Book. But many Scots agreed with English Puritans, and did not want to be ordered about over religion.

The picture shows what happened in Edinburgh Cathedral on the first Sunday the Prayer Book was supposed to be used. Those are stools flying through the air at the bishop. There was trouble all over Scotland.

Charles had another unpopular minister, the Earl of Strafford. He ruled Ireland for the King very efficiently. Many people feared the Earl of Strafford. They were afraid he might help the King to become too strong. Perhaps then Charles would rule without Parliament altogether.

The Scots felt so strongly they decided to fight. Now Charles had landed himself with a war he could not pay for. He had some soldiers, but they were unpaid and badly equipped, and they did not want to fight the Scots. They ran away when a battle looked likely.

By 1640, Charles could only do one thing – call Parliament, and hope they would agree to give him the money he needed to pay for a proper army. But MPs were not going to forget the last 11 years. They were determined to stop Charles ruling without them. This Parliament lasted a long time, and is always called the Long Parliament.

The Long Parliament

Members of Parliament could now make Charles do what they wanted. They imprisoned Archbishop Laud, and accused the Earl of Strafford of high treason. When Charles refused to agree to Strafford's execution, there was a riot outside Whitehall Palace. Violent crowds shouted threats at Charles's unpopular Queen, Henrietta Maria. Charles gave in to save his beloved wife, and Strafford was beheaded.

Parliament stopped ship money, and the other ways Charles got money without asking them. They passed a law saying there *must* be a Parliament every three years, whether the King wanted it or not. They began to ask for more and more. Some MPs began to worry that things were going too far.

The Five Members

Henrietta Maria kept telling Charles to act strongly. She told him he ought to arrest John Pym, John Hampden, and three other important MPs. 'Go pull those rogues out by the ears, or never see my face again!' she is supposed to have said.

On 4 January 1642, Charles set out from Whitehall with 300 soldiers. It was only five minutes' march to Parliament, but the five leaders had been warned. They quickly escaped by river, to the City of London. Most people there supported them, and they would be safe. Meanwhile Charles and his soldiers arrived at the front of the Parliament buildings. Charles walked into the House of Commons, leaving his soldiers by the doorway. He looked for the Five Members – but they were nowhere to be seen. He said: 'I see the birds have flown', and asked the Speaker ←74 where they were. The Speaker knelt before the King and replied:

> May it please Your Majesty, I have neither eyes to see nor tongue to speak in this place but as this House is pleased to direct me, whose servant I am here, and I humbly beg Your Majesty's pardon that I cannot give any answer than this.

So the King had to leave without the five men he had come to arrest. He had tried force, and it had not worked. London was in an uproar. It was too dangerous for the King to stay there. He went north to start collecting an army together. The Five Members returned in triumph to Parliament. They and their supporters also started to train and equip soldiers. War soon began.

John Pym was a leader of the MPs in the Long Parliament. He was a clever lawyer, and led the attack on Charles I very skilfully.

Steps to war

1625	Charles I became King. He married Henrietta Maria
1629	Charles decided to rule without Parliament
1635	Charles asked for ship money
1637	John Hampden's trial. The Scots refused to accept the English Prayer Book and went to war
1640	The Long Parliament
1642	Charles tried to arrest the Five Members. War between King and Parliament began

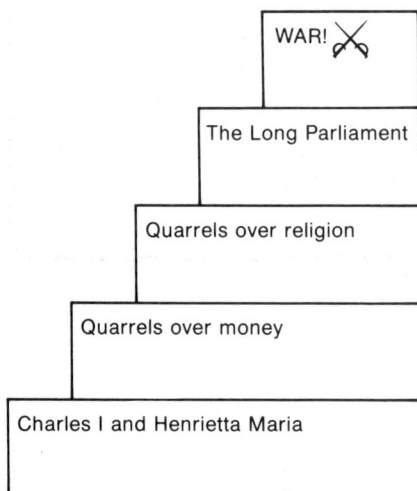

1 Write out what the Speaker said to the King in modern English. Why do you think he was so polite?

2 You are a reporter who was in the House of Commons when the message warning the Five Members was received. Write a newspaper report with headlines describing how Charles tried to arrest the Five Members. Start with the message.

3 Copy the step diagram in the margin. Take about half a page. Add a sentence or two to explain each step.

88

Ciuitatis Westmonasteriensis pars

Parlament House   the Hall   the Abby

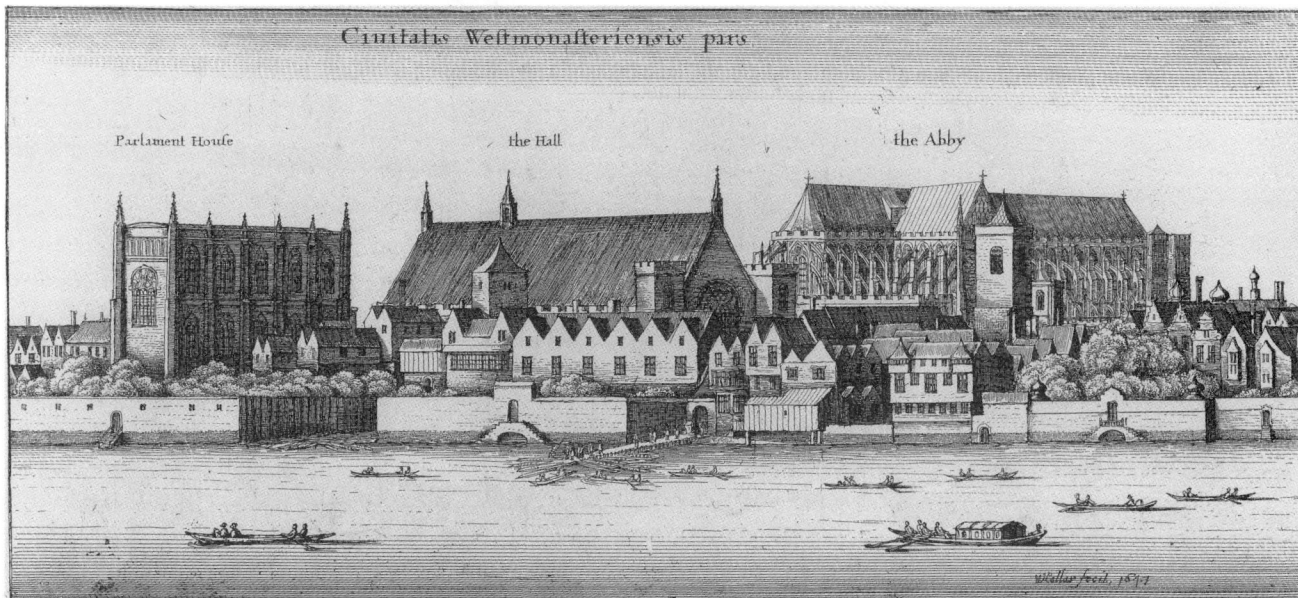

Charles I and his soldiers had to march to Parliament House on the left of his picture, when he came to arrest the Five Members. Whitehall Palace is only just out of the picture on the right. The Five Members escaped from the *doorway facing on to the river where you can see the boats waiting. This picture of Westminster in Charles I's time should help you to see how quickly they had to make their escape.*

■ Use the map on page 76 to make your own sketch map of London and Westminster. Mark in the King's route from Whitehall to Parliament, and the five members' escape route to the City of London. Use two different colours, and a key.

Key words in this chapter to help you remember and understand what you have learnt. You should be able to use these words now and find evidence in the chapter which illustrates them.

James I	**Pilgrim Fathers**	**Charles I**
undignified	Puritans	artistic
clumsy	*Mayflower*	religious
divine right of kings	New Plymouth	marriage
peace	Massachusetts	Parliament
tobacco	native Americans	Ship Money
Gunpowder Plot	Indians	Church of England
plotters	settlers	laws
treason	colony	riot
	disease	The Five Members
	food supplies	escape
	Thanksgiving	

7 Cavaliers and Roundheads

A civil war is a war when people in the same country fight each other. The English Civil War began in 1642 and lasted until 1646. It split up families and friends, and brought a great deal of suffering and unhappiness.

The two sides

This cartoon of 1642 shows the two sides at the beginning of the war already had the nicknames which we still use. Like most nicknames they were not meant to be kind and polite.

Cavaliers were the King's supporters – the Royalists. They believed they must be loyal to the King, even if they did not always approve of everything he did.

People on Parliament's side called them Cavaliers. The name meant a wild cruel horseman who killed and stole. Not all Cavaliers were like that. But soldiers on both sides sometimes behaved badly.

Roundheads supported Parliament. They believed there was only one way to make Charles rule with Parliament. They must fight and defeat him, to make him give in.

Charles I's Queen, Henrietta Maria may have given Roundheads their name. Just before the war, she looked out of the windows of Whitehall Palace at a crowd of Londoners jeering and cat-calling. They were mostly ordinary working people with short hair, so the Queen thought their heads looked round. Some Puritans wore short hair ← 82 , and most Puritans supported Parliament. But there were rich people on Parliament's side too, and they usually wore their hair long because it was fashionable. So not all Roundheads had 'round heads'.

1 Which side is which in the cartoon? How do you know?

2 Cavaliers and Roundheads made the best of their nicknames. But nicknames can hurt. Should we avoid them?

Divided families

Sir Edmund Verney was a country gentleman with a large family of ten children. He lived in Buckinghamshire. He was very unhappy when the war broke out, and we know how he felt because he told a friend, Edward Hyde, who wrote down what he said. Sir Edmund said that he was very depressed, because he really wanted the King to agree to rule with Parliament. On the other hand, he had served the King for almost 30 years, and could not betray him now. So he must fight for the King – but he was sure he would be killed.

Sir Edmund had another reason to be depressed. This letter shows why. It was written by his third son 'Mun' (short for Edmund) to the eldest in the family, Ralph, in 1642:

> Brother, what I feared is proved true, which is your being against the King . . . It grieves my heart to think that my father and I who so dearly love you . . . should be your enemy . . . I am so much troubled to think of you being on the side you are that I can write no more, only I shall pray for peace.

1 Which of the two brothers is a Roundhead? Which is a Cavalier?

2 What does this letter tell you about how they got on?

The Verney family had a hard time in the war. Sir Edmund Verney was killed in the first big battle, Edgehill. Things became so difficult for Ralph and his wife that he went abroad, but he had to leave his children behind. Mun was killed in Ireland in 1649. Two daughters who married during the war both lost their husbands in the fighting.

Lucy Hutchinson was married to a Roundhead colonel. She wrote her husband John's life story after the war. As the war started, their home was surrounded by Cavalier soldiers, and John had to escape quickly. Lucy said she was 'somewhat afflicted to be left so alone.' (That was probably putting it mildly.) But she found the officer in charge of the Cavaliers was her own brother Allan. The meeting seems to have been quite a happy one.

■ In pairs, work out the conversation that Lucy and her brother might have had when they met.

A lot of people tried to avoid taking sides altogether. If they were lucky, they lived in a place where there was no fighting. In that case, they could usually keep out of it all. Probably only one person in every 40 joined the Cavalier or Roundhead armies.

Sir Edmund Verney's ring. Sir Edmund carried the King's standard (there is a picture of it on page 92) at the Battle of Edgehill and died defending it. When Cavalier soldiers recaptured it, they found that Sir Edmund's hand had been cut off and was still gripping the flagpole. On one finger was this ring, with a picture of the King on it.

The King raised his standard (a flag with the Royal crest) at Nottingham in August 1642. This was a sign for all loyal subjects to join him. The picture above was printed to spread the news. The weather was bad and the standard soon blew down – which some people thought was a sign of bad luck.

The two sides in 1642

	Cavaliers	Roundheads
Places	Mainly the north of England, Wales and the west	Mainly the south and east
	Some important cities: e.g. York, Oxford, Nottingham, Shrewsbury	The capital, London, with its large population, its wealth and trade
		Several ports: e.g. Hull, Plymouth, Bristol
People	75 per cent of the nobility	25 per cent of the nobility
	Gentry and rich merchants fairly evenly divided	
		Craftsmen, shopkeepers and traders, mostly in the towns
	Country people tended to follow the local gentry	
Fighting men	Better horse soldiers (cavalry)	Not such a strong army The navy helped to bring in supplies
	More gold and silver plate to melt down for cash	

■ On page 93 is some information about Oxford and York. Match this information up with the King's needs. Copy the table below. Decide which information fits Need 1, and write the letter for that information in the correct box. Do the same for Needs 2, 3 and 4. Give a score out of 5 for each need. Need 3 has been completed to help you.

When you have done this, add up the marks for York and Oxford. Decide whether you think that the King was right to choose Oxford. Give your reasons.

Needs	York	Oxford
1		
2		
3	B, D 2	B, D, 5
4		
Total		

Need 3

York scores 2 because it's close to Hull, but far from London
Oxford scores 5 because it's on the Thames and close to London

Choosing a headquarters

The King had lost London before the war even started. So he had to choose a headquarters which he could use as his capital. This is what he needed:

Need 1   Must be easy to defend.
Need 2   Must have plenty of Royalist supporters.
Need 3   Must be a good centre – easy to send in supplies, and not too far from London which he wanted to win back.
Need 4   Must be large and rich enough to provide room for the court, and to supply the army which would be based there.

The King chose Oxford. He might have chosen several other places, including York.

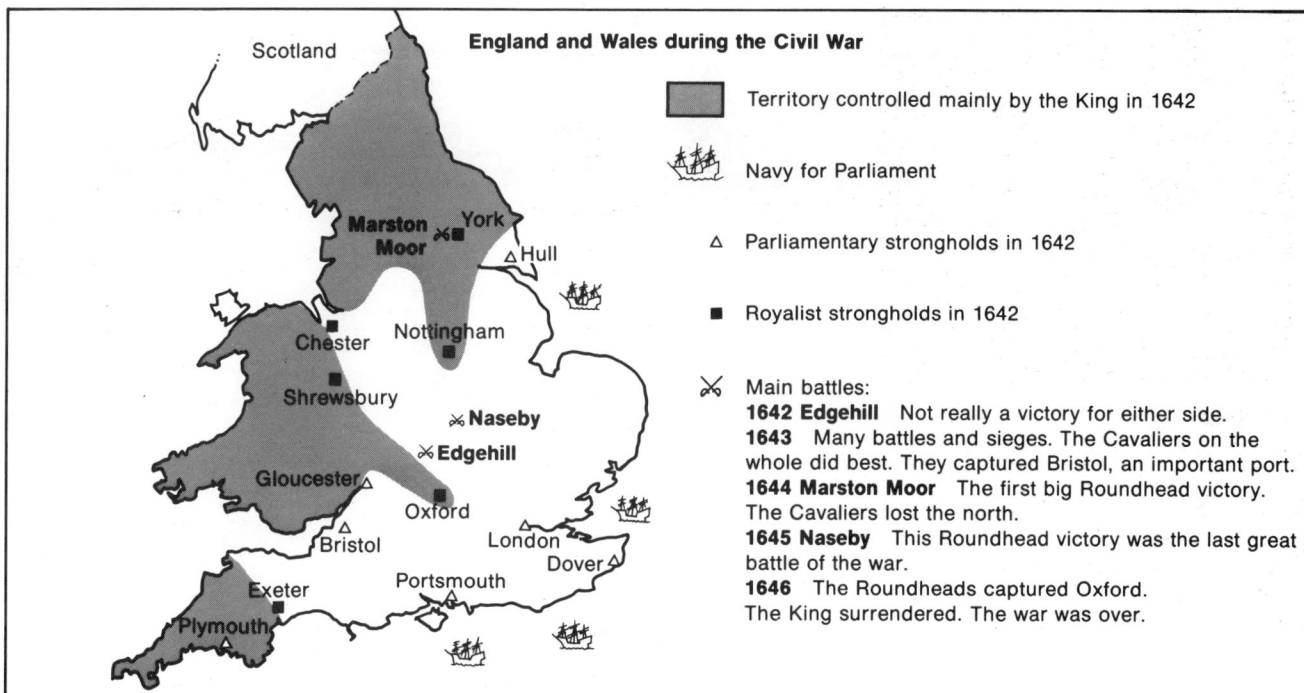

England and Wales during the Civil War

Territory controlled mainly by the King in 1642

Navy for Parliament

△ Parliamentary strongholds in 1642

■ Royalist strongholds in 1642

✗ Main battles:
1642 Edgehill Not really a victory for either side.
1643 Many battles and sieges. The Cavaliers on the whole did best. They captured Bristol, an important port.
1644 Marston Moor The first big Roundhead victory. The Cavaliers lost the north.
1645 Naseby This Roundhead victory was the last great battle of the war.
1646 The Roundheads captured Oxford. The King surrendered. The war was over.

York	Oxford
A Some important people in the surrounding area were on opposite sides. The Fairfax family was on Parliament's side, but the greatest landowner, the Earl of Newcastle, was Royalist.	**A** Some landowners in the surrounding area were for Parliament (e.g. Lord Saye and Sele, near Banbury). The rich and powerful university was Royalist. It more or less controlled the city – but many ordinary citizens supported Parliament.
B An important trading city on the River Ouse. But its nearby port, Hull was in the hands of Parliament	**B** An important trading city. On the River Thames, which was used a great deal for transport of goods.
C The city had four miles of strong walls.	**C** The walled city lay between the River Thames and the River Cherwell.
D About 200 miles from London.	**D** About 50 miles from London.
E The capital of the North. The King spent some time there just before the war started.	**E** The university had many fine and roomy college buildings. The colleges were rich; most of them owned precious gold and silver.

1 Give at least two reasons why the King decided he must put all his efforts into winning back London.

2 Give as many reasons as you can find on these two pages why the King had to win the war quickly, if he was going to win it at all.

This picture shows the first battle of the war – Edgehill. It is all rather too tidy, but it tells us a good deal about Civil War soldiers.

Soldiers and weapons

The **cavalry** (horse soldiers) are fighting fiercely in the background. Horses were expensive, and cavalry were the crack troops in an army. At Edgehill, the Cavalier cavalry began the battle with a terrifying charge. The Roundhead army nearly broke up. But Prince Rupert, the Cavalier commander, could not stop his horsemen, and they galloped right off the battlefield to loot a nearby village. The Roundheads had time to recover. The rest of the battle was mostly a desperate fight on foot which nobody really won.

Musketeers had a difficult job. At the beginning of the war, their muskets (a gun about the size of a modern rifle) were so heavy that they had to prop them up on stands. Later muskets became lighter and stands were no longer needed. Muskets sometimes failed to fire, and it took about a minute to load them – a long time when a cavalry charge is thundering down on you. Find the musketeers at Edgehill.

Pikemen had to be tall and strong. They carried very long pikes (like spears), measuring about 4 metres. They had to hold their pikes firmly against a cavalry charge. Then they had to advance with pikes lowered; this was called 'push of pike'. There are lots of pikemen in the picture.

Cannons were heavy and difficult to move. They used about 1300 kilos of shot in a battle. They could cause a lot of damage, but still often missed their target. There were cannon at Edgehill, though they are not in the picture.

Find the **standards** (flags) in the picture. There are lots. Soldiers did not all wear the same uniform, and had to be able to recognise their own side – and keep together, near their standard. They shouted passwords too. At the battle of Naseby, Cavaliers shouted 'Queen Mary', and Roundheads 'God our strength'. Battles were

A musketeer. He wears flasks of powder strung on his sash. He has to ram the powder down the barrel of the musket. How can you tell this is a musketeer at the beginning of the war?

94

noisy and confusing. Smoke from muskets and cannons could make it difficult to see. Soldiers did not always know what was going on.

Armour was usually just a breast and back plate which protected the body to the waist. Soldiers wore a buff coat underneath. This was a long coat or sleeveless tunic made of very thick ox-hide (leather) which was oiled to make it soft. The sides were slit so it was easy to move. Some soldiers did not wear their armour. Lucy Hutchinson worried about her husband:

> He put off a very good suit of armour that he had which, being musket-proof, was so heavy that it heated him, and so could not be persuaded to wear anything but a buff-coat.

The wounded You did not have much chance if you were seriously wounded in a seventeenth-century battle. This is a letter from the Roundhead commander Oliver Cromwell to his friend Colonel Walton after the battle of Marston Moor:

> Sir, God hath taken away your eldest son by a cannon shot. It brake his leg. We were necessitated to have it cut off, whereof he died . . . There is your precious child, full of glory, never to know sin or sorrow any more. He was a gallant young man.

This young man was an officer, and a surgeon looked after him. You know what operations were like before anaesthetics; people were lucky to survive them. ← 20 Ordinary soldiers were often just left wounded on the battlefield. Sometimes that saved them. A wounded soldier at Edgehill, left on the battlefield all night, thought he did not bleed to death because it was so cold that the frost made his blood clot.

Women like Lucy Hutchinson often went to war with their men. They were usually good at nursing, for they did it at home. There were hardly any hospitals then. Lucy took her own special ointments with her, and the wounded soldiers in her care recovered. She insisted on looking after wounded Cavaliers as well as Roundheads.

Later in the war, Roundhead cavalry wore helmets like this. Work out why this was a good design to protect the head of an active fighting man in a battle.

1 Make an illustrated list of the following. Explain how each was used, and any advantages and disadvantages:
- Cavalry • Muskets • Pikes • Cannons • Armour
- Buffcoats • Standards

2 The soldier on the right meets the farmer who owns most of his loot. Write the conversation which follows. (How would the soldier explain himself?)

3 Make a list of the things you would dislike if you were a seventeenth-century soldier. Is there anything you would like?

Soldiers were usually paid less than farm labourers, and very often there was no money to pay them at all. They had to find their own food, and often could not afford to pay for it. How do you think this soldier has solved the problem? What kind of things has he managed to get hold of? People did not like having soldiers in their home area. This cartoon shows one reason why.

Villagers and townspeople

A Roundhead cartoon showing Cavaliers up to all kinds of dreadful behaviour. How can you tell they are Cavaliers? In fact both sides could behave badly, but on the whole commanders tried to stop them.

Villagers from Charlescombe, near Bath, sent a bill to Parliament in 1646. They had not been paid for the time in 1643 when a Roundhead army had been in their village. They claimed:

← 2

For hay, grass and wood	£10
William Maynard's bill for bread, beer, hay and grass and wood	£5 5s 6d
Soldiers' lodging with villagers	£9 9s 6d

1 What do you think William Maynard's job probably was?

2 Make a list of the things the troops used which they had not paid for. What kind of troops were they? Which things might cause the villagers most hardship?

Oxford was a busy crowded city in peacetime. When the King made it his headquarters, it became crowded to bursting. We know that in one small part of the city there were 74 houses. In those houses were 408 *extra* people. These are some of the problems people who lived in Oxford had to cope with in the war:

Disease There were serious 'plagues' in 1644 and 1645. Probably it was typhus. Soldiers and townspeople died.
Fire There was a bad fire in 1644, started by a soldier roasting a pig he had stolen. Over 200 houses were burnt.
Law and order So many people got drunk that the King ordered the inns to close in the evenings. There was a gibbet in the centre of the town to hang criminals.

These problems hit many towns where armies came, even when there was no actual fighting. If a town was attacked, then things were worse still.

■ Make a list of the problems an Oxford family in a two-roomed house would have, when they have four extra soldiers living with them.

Women in wartime

The war changed the lives of many women. Some of them, like Lucy Hutchinson, went to war with their husbands. Often wives stayed at home to keep things going. If there was fighting in the area, sometimes they had to turn into soldiers.

Brilliana, Lady Harley was one of these women. Her husband was a busy Roundhead MP and had to stay in London. She was a gentle person, not used to managing on her own. Seven hundred Cavalier troops surrounded her home, Brampton Bryan Castle, near Hereford. The house was cut off – it was a siege.

The Cavaliers sent a trumpeter to tell Brilliana to surrender. She refused, although she knew she was risking her own safety, and her children and servants. She told the Cavaliers that her husband trusted her to defend their home. She said:

> I do not know that it is his pleasure that I should entertain soldiers in his house.

The Cavaliers built earth banks so near the house that the people inside could hear the soldiers' 'rotten language'. The King wrote to Brilliana telling her to give in. She refused. Then after a month, a Roundhead army marched into the area, and drove off the Cavaliers.

The danger was not over. The Roundheads could not stay, and soon the Cavaliers were back, and the siege began again. Just at this desperate moment, Brilliana fell ill and died. She had remained calm and cheerful right to the end. All her household were full of 'sighs and tears', for they loved her dearly. The castle fell to the enemy. The Cavaliers looked after Brilliana's three small children, but her husband lost goods worth £13 000, and did not get his house back until the end of the war.

1 Make a strip cartoon of the wartime adventures of Brilliana.

2 Design a ballad sheet which tells the story of a girl who joined the army. If you cannot manage a poem, design it as a strip cartoon.

Wartime ballad sheets sometimes told stories of women joining the army. This one is called 'The Female Warrior'. It told the story of a girl who became a drummer 'boy' – until she had a baby!

Prince Rupert

Prince Rupert was the best soldier the Cavaliers had. He was brave and dashing, and a brilliant cavalry commander. He seemed to know just where the enemy was, and how to catch him. (But he sometimes let his horsemen get out of control, as at Edgehill.) ← 94

Rupert had a big white hunting dog called 'Boy' who went everywhere with him – even into battle. The Roundheads soon began to feel they could never defeat Rupert, and they thought his dog put a spell on them.

At last, at Marston Moor in 1644 ← 93 , the Roundheads defeated Rupert for the first time. Boy was killed, and Rupert had to escape from the battlefield. This Roundhead cartoon was printed soon after, and makes out that Rupert had to hide in a beanfield in a very undignified way. (That may not be true.) It shows Roundhead soldiers capturing his luggage. Can you find Boy?

Prince Rupert was the King's nephew. He was only 23 when this portrait was painted at the beginning of the war. But although he was so young, he had already fought in a war in Germany, and knew more about fighting than the rest of the King's generals. They were sometimes jealous of him. Rupert was a typical Cavalier, with his long hair and good looks.

1 How does the cartoon tell you where the battle of Marston Moor was fought?

2 What are the soldiers finding in Rupert's luggage? Why did the Roundheads put these things in the picture? (*Clue* Rupert was not a Catholic. But the Roundheads often said Cavaliers were Catholics ← 82, 85 .)

3 What colour was Boy? Why is he a different colour here?

4 Act an imaginary scene just after the battle: Rupert is back in Oxford, talking to another officer about the defeat. His servant brings in this cartoon, which he has just bought from a ballad seller. What does Rupert say?

Oliver Cromwell and the Ironsides

Oliver Cromwell was the man who, more than anyone else, defeated Prince Rupert at Marston Moor. At the beginning of the war, he was an ordinary country gentleman, who lived in Huntingdonshire. He was a very strong Puritan and a member of the Long Parliament ←88. He firmly supported John Pym. He fought in the battle of Edgehill, and was very worried about the Roundhead army. He told his cousin John Hampden ←86 that Roundhead soldiers were just not good enough to beat the King.

The Ironsides

Cromwell went home to Huntingdonshire, and began to train his own cavalry. He was determined it would be good enough to win the war. He was so successful that his troops soon got the nickname 'Ironsides', because they were solid as iron in a battle. This is how he did it:

- He picked his men carefully, especially the officers. He wanted 'godly, honest men'. He meant strict Puritans, who believed like he did that God would give them victory. He said he would rather have a plainly dressed captain who 'knows what he fights for, and loves what he knows' than a grand gentleman. Then, he said, honest men will obey him.

- He was strict with his troops. They were punished for swearing (a fine of 12d, half a day's pay), and were put in the stocks if they got drunk. They had to obey orders without question.

- He trained them carefully. His cavalry learnt to charge at a 'round trot'. This was fast enough to break through the enemy, but not so fast that they got out of control. Cromwell's Ironsides never charged off the battlefield like Rupert's troops did at Edgehill.

- He cared for his troops. 'I have a lovely company', he said proudly of them. He always did his best to see they were paid too.

- He always chose the right moment in a battle to attack, and he won every battle he fought.

Cromwell's Ironsides became part of the **New Model Army** in 1645. This was the first army organised over the whole country. The New Model Army won the battle of Naseby. Though the war dragged on until 1646, Naseby was the final defeat for the King and the Cavaliers.

This portrait of Cromwell was painted after the war, when he was the most important man in England. But it gives us a good idea of 'Old Ironsides', as Rupert nicknamed him. The name stuck to his troops too.
Cromwell was not good-looking, but he did not mind. There is a story that he told a painter to put all the warts and pimples on his face into his picture, or he would not pay him for it. He has certainly got some pimples in this portrait.

■ You are a shopkeeper in Cromwell's home town of Huntingdon, and a firm Puritan. Write a letter to your wife explaining how pleased you are that Cromwell has chosen you as one of his officers, and why you have joined the Ironsides. Use the information on this page carefully.

1642 Edgehill	A victory for no one
1644 Marston Moor	Victory for Parliament
1645 Naseby	Victory for Parliament

The chief judge in the court which tried Charles I was a lawyer called John Bradshaw. He was not very well known or important. He wore this bullet-proof hat all through the trial. Who was he afraid of?

Trial and execution

Charles I soon became a prisoner of the New Model Army. But he still believed that he was the King, appointed by God. Although he was a prisoner, he managed to make a secret deal with the Scots, and a second civil war began in 1648. It was very short, and a disaster for the Cavaliers. Cromwell and the Army soon defeated them.

Cromwell and the Army leaders decided Charles must die. They put him on trial. No one had put a King on trial before, and no one knew quite how to do it. A special court was set up. One hundred and thirty-five judges were appointed, but only about a third of them turned up. Charles was accused of being a traitor to the people of England, and of starting the war.

The King said no one could put him on trial. He refused to defend himself. He wore his hat the whole time to show he did not have any respect for this court.

The trial lasted from 20 to 27 January 1649. Charles I was found guilty, and sentenced to death by execution. This is the death warrant which ordered the execution to take place. It is signed by the judges at the trial.

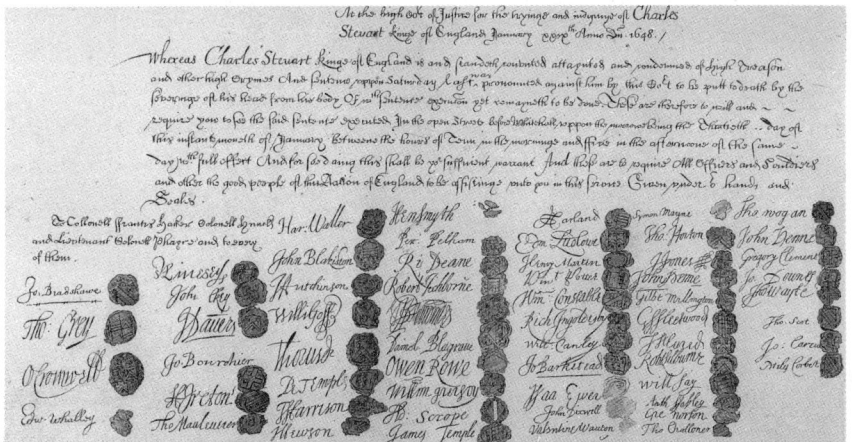

The death warrant ordering the execution of Charles I.

1 Find the signatures of John Bradshaw and Oliver Cromwell on the death warrant. How many signatures are there altogether? How many should there be?

2 Stage a class trial of Charles I. Make it like a modern trial. Put Charles in the witness box. Lawyers for the prosecution and defence question him. You could have witnesses too: John Hampden, Oliver Cromwell, Sir Edmund Verney and Henrietta Maria. Then take a class vote on whether Charles should die.

30 January 1649

On this bitterly cold January morning, the King woke early. He was completely calm. He told his servant that this was like his second marriage day. He said: 'I fear not death. Death is not terrible to me.' He put on two shirts, so that he would not shiver with cold, and seem afraid. At about 10 o'clock, soldiers took him to his beautiful Banqueting House in Whitehall Palace, which he had not seen for seven years. Outside there was a huge silent crowd, and soldiers everywhere.

It was nearly 2 o'clock when the King stepped out on the scaffold. Two disguised executioners waited for him. Nobody knows who they were, even now. Charles made a short speech, which only the people near him on the scaffold could hear. Before he put his head on the block, he said one last word: 'Remember'. The axe fell.

The execution of the King

A

A picture printed soon after the execution outside the Banqueting House of Whitehall Palace. Can you find a clue that the artist is not English? Although he probably did not see the execution, he knew about the crowds who watched. Who is cheering? How do other people feel?

B Part of Charles I's speech on the scaffold:

All the world knows I never did begin a war first with the two Houses of Parliament. ... [the people's] liberty and freedom consists in having government ... It is not for having a share in government ... A subject and a sovereign are clear different things ... therefore I tell you that I am a martyr of the people.

C A 17-year-old boy's eye-witness account:

The Blow I saw given with a sad heart, and at that instant there was such a groan by the thousands then present, as I never heard before, and desire I may never hear again. There was ... one troop immediately marching to Westminster, and another from Westminster, to confuse the people and scatter them, so that I had much ado to escape home without hurt.

1 Write down the meaning of: traitor ← 63, martyr ← 57.

2 Find evidence which tells you:
   a) that the judges at Charles I's trial were frightened.
   b) that the Army expected trouble at the execution.
   c) that many people did not want Charles to die.
   d) that Charles still believed he was right.

3 Write an eye-witness account by a Roundhead or a Cavalier of the execution of Charles I. (Think how they would use the words in question 1.)

This is the first page of a book of prayers – people said they were written by Charles I. The book was already being sold in London on the day of the execution. It shows Charles as a martyr. His royal crown is on the ground, and he is holding a crown of thorns, like Jesus. In Heaven, a martyr's crown is ready for him. Many people remembered Charles like this, even if they had not agreed with all his actions.

Oliver Cromwell, Lord Protector

Now England was a republic, a country without a king. Charles II (Charles I's son) had escaped and was in Holland – hoping that one day he would be king. Oliver Cromwell and his Army held the power. First Cromwell had to be sure there were no attacks from outside, especially through England's two 'back doors' – Ireland and Scotland.

Ireland

Cromwell crushed Catholic Ireland. He was not usually cruel, but he was determined there would be no more trouble. When he besieged Drogheda in 1649, his soldiers set fire to the church steeple which was full of soldiers. When the rest surrendered, he reported that:

> their officers were knocked on the head, and every tenth man of the soldiers killed; and the rest shipped to Barbados [in the West Indies] . . . I am persuaded this is the righteous judgment of God upon these barbarous wretches.

Cromwell made sure that his Army stayed in control of Ireland. He took land belonging to 8000 Catholic landowners and gave it to his soldiers and supporters.

Scotland

The Scots supported Charles II, so Cromwell marched north to deal with them. He won the battle of Dunbar. The next year, 1651, Charles II invaded England with a Scots army. Cromwell won his last great victory, the battle of Worcester. A few Cavaliers managed to escape, including the young Charles II. He spent six weeks on the run. A reward of £1000 was offered for 'a tall young man two yards high, with hair deep brown, near to black'. No one betrayed Charles to get the reward, but nobody fought for him either. He had to escape abroad again. Scotland became an occupied country, ruled by England.

King Oliver?

In 1653, Oliver Cromwell became Lord Protector. That meant he was the ruler of England. He wanted to rule with Parliament. But he had the same problems as Charles I. Parliament grumbled, and did not agree to enough taxes to run the country, and to pay for the Army, which cost a lot of money. Cromwell sent the MPs home.

Then in 1655 Cromwell divided the country into 11 districts. An Army general ruled each district. They made strict rules for everyone; they closed pubs, and stopped horse-racing. (London theatres were already closed.) They behaved like real Puritans.

Most of them were. But they also stopped these things because they meant crowds, and crowds often meant trouble. The generals were very unpopular.

In the end, Parliament asked Cromwell to be king. They probably thought everyone would feel more secure then. But Cromwell refused. He knew most of the soldiers in his beloved Army would never forgive him if he accepted.

The country remained peaceful. Cromwell did not allow people to be persecuted for their religion. Countries in Europe respected him, and did not help Charles II to win back his crown.

But by 1658, Cromwell was a sad old man. His favourite daughter died. Then he fell ill. On 3 September, the date of his victories at Dunbar and Worcester, Cromwell died.

The world turned upside down

When King Charles I was executed, people felt the world was upside down, and they did not know what would happen next. This picture was printed then. Everything is upside down. At the bottom, a mouse chases a cat, and a rabbit chases a dog.

1 Write down all the things which are upside down in this picture.

2 Design your own poster, dated 1649, called 'The World Turned Upside Down'. Include a crown and a church.

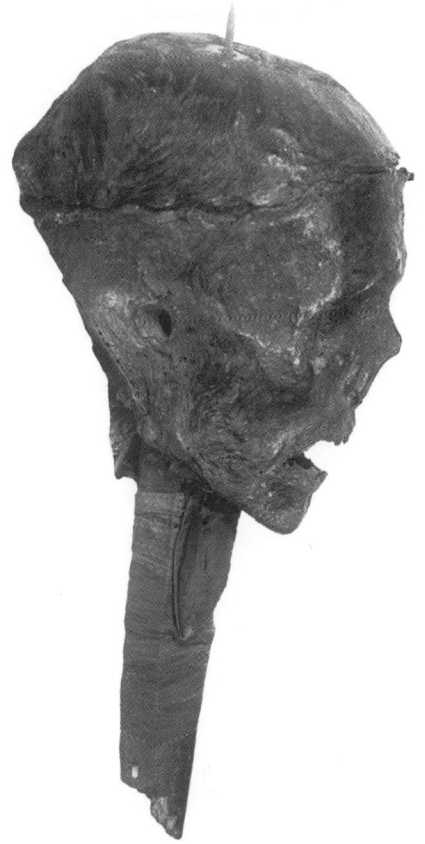

When Cromwell died, his funeral was like a king's, and he was buried in Westminster Abbey. But his body did not stay there. When Charles II returned, the corpse was dug up, the head cut off, and stuck up on a gallows at Tyburn. Later it became part of a peepshow at a fair. This photograph was taken before it was buried in this century at Sidney Sussex College, Cambridge, where Cromwell was a student.

Nobody knew quite what to do. The world still seemed upside down. Oliver's son, Richard became Protector for a while. But he did not last long. In the end, there seemed only one thing to do: to have a king again. In 1660, Charles II returned to England to rule the country.

1 Discuss in class what you think of Cromwell, and work out a list of good and bad things about him.

2 Write a few sentences in your own words about each of these headings:
    The execution of the King
    Oliver Cromwell and Ireland
    The Battles of Dunbar and Worcester
    Oliver Cromwell, Lord Protector
    Cromwell's death

The Stuart Family

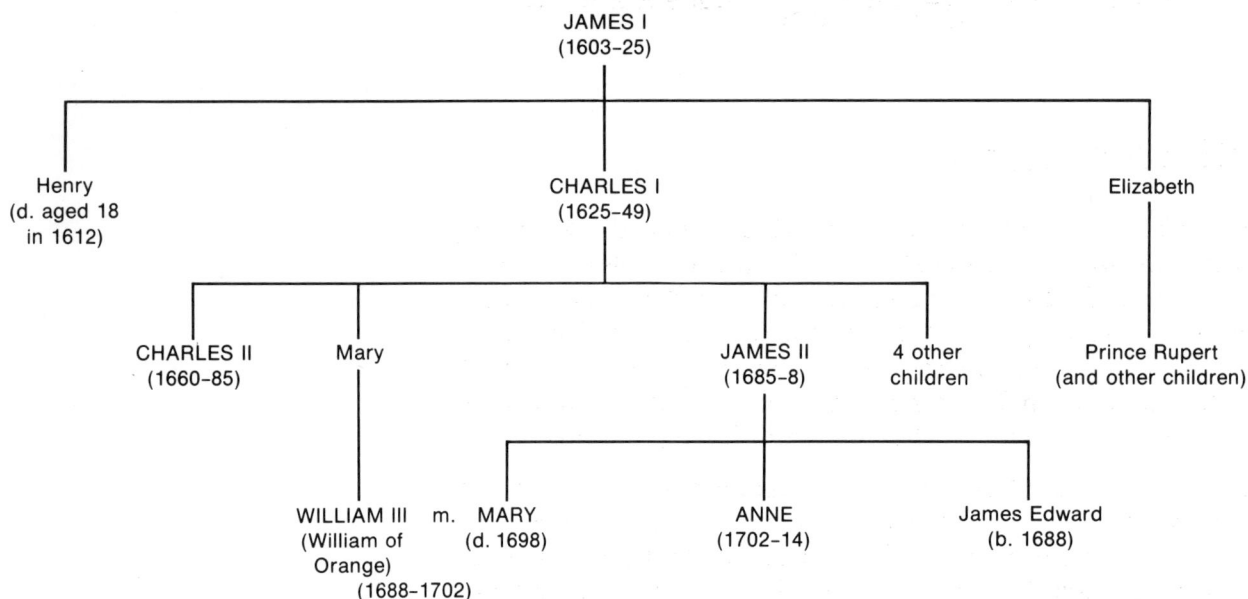

```
                          JAMES I
                         (1603–25)
        ┌────────────────────┼────────────────────────────┐
      Henry              CHARLES I                      Elizabeth
   (d. aged 18           (1625–49)
    in 1612)
        ┌──────────┬────────────────┬──────────┐            │
   CHARLES II     Mary          JAMES II    4 other    Prince Rupert
   (1660–85)                    (1685–8)    children  (and other children)
            ┌────────────────┬──────────────────┐
      WILLIAM III  m.  MARY        ANNE        James Edward
      (William of    (d. 1698)   (1702–14)      (b. 1688)
       Orange)
      (1688–1702)
```

REIGNING SOVEREIGNS ARE IN CAPITAL LETTERS
The dates of their reigns are shown by their names

Key words in this section to help you remember and understand what you have learnt. You should be able to use these words now and find evidence in the chapter which illustrates each of them.

Cavaliers and Roundheads	Wartime	Death of Charles I	Oliver Cromwell
officers	battle	trial	Ireland
cavalry	siege	court	Scotland
musketeers	charge	guilty	Protector
pikemen	surrender	death warrant	generals
cannon	medical care	execution	military rule
standards	loot	traitor	
breastplate	Ironsides	martyr	
helmet	New Model Army		
buff coat			

8 Changing times

Different rulers

Charles II came back to England to be King in 1660. He was a witty, clever man, who was good at hiding his feelings. Eleven difficult years of exile had taught him that. He wanted to enjoy himself now he was King. He did too: his pleasures included gambling, the theatre and horse-racing. He had several mistresses and 14 illegitimate children. He was certainly not a Puritan! But he knew he had to do two things if he wanted to keep his crown.

He had to rule with Parliament – who kept him short of money, so he had to keep in with MPs. He also had to support the Church of England. People were tired of the Puritans. And they still hated and feared Catholics. The Church of England seemed safe.
← 59

Charles would probably have liked to do without Parliament. He wanted to stop quarrels over religion; he may even have wanted to be a Catholic. But he wanted to stay as King of England even more. He managed to keep out of real trouble.

A Catholic king

Charles died of a stroke in 1685. He had no legal children, so his brother James became the next King. He was very different. He was a firm Catholic and very open about it – which was both brave and stupid! He never seemed to realise how much his religion upset his subjects, and he started to make England into a Catholic country. He also soon made it clear he was not going to take any notice of Parliament.

For a time people waited to see what would happen. James was quite old, and he had two daughters, Mary and Anne, who were Protestant. Perhaps he would not last very long. But in 1688, his Queen had a son, James Edward. He would be brought up a Catholic – and become the next King. It was too much. Seven important men in Parliament asked William of Orange, the Dutch husband of James's eldest daughter, Mary, to come to England.

Revolution

In November 1688, William landed with an army. Nobody tried to stop him. Many of the officers in James's army came to join him. So did James's younger daughter Anne. James and his family escaped to France. He never came back. William and Mary became joint King and Queen. It was a revolution without any fighting.

■ Draw the family tree on page 104. Underneath answer these questions:
a) What relation are these people to each other:
Charles II and James II?
James II and the two Marys?
James II and William of Orange? ◁4◁▭
b) Which child of James II should have been the next ruler? Why did English people not want this child to rule? ◁4◁▭
c) Write a sentence saying what happened on each of these dates:
1660, 1685, 1688. ◁3◁▭

New rulers and new promises

The powerful men in the English Parliament had got rid of one King. William and Mary were only allowed to become the next rulers if they made some promises. Most of these were in a famous law passed by Parliament in 1689: the **Bill of Rights**. The rest were agreed soon after:

- The monarch must not be a Catholic, or marry a Catholic
- Parliament must make the laws
- Parliament must control how taxes are spent
- Parliament must agree if an army is needed
- Parliament must meet every 3 years (3 was soon changed to 7)

■ Copy out these promises. Find out if they are still laws now. ◁✏

After this, no King could rule England like Charles I or James II had tried to do. But Kings still had power. So did the rich landowners in Parliament. Ordinary men and women still did not sit in Parliament, or have any power. Just about 200 years later, long after the time covered in this book, they began to win power too. That is another important story.

These changes happened in England and Wales. But they soon made a difference in Ireland and Scotland too.

Wales

Wales was part of England, with the same law courts and counties. But the Welsh language did not die, and many Welsh people did not want much to do with the English.

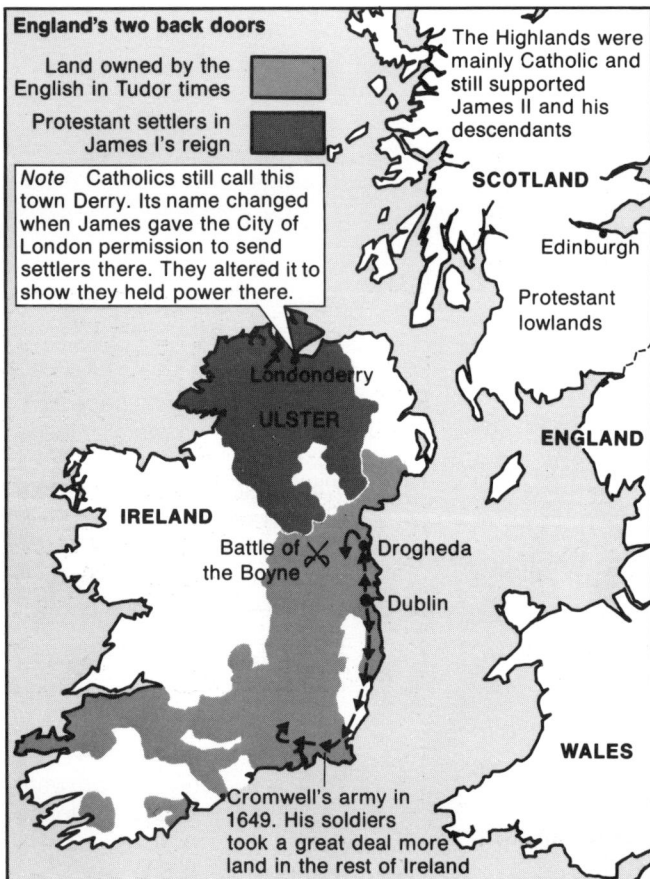

England's two back doors

Land owned by the English in Tudor times

Protestant settlers in James I's reign

Note Catholics still call this town Derry. Its name changed when James gave the City of London permission to send settlers there. They altered it to show they held power there.

The Highlands were mainly Catholic and still supported James II and his descendants

SCOTLAND

Edinburgh

Protestant lowlands

Londonderry

ULSTER

ENGLAND

IRELAND

Battle of the Boyne

Drogheda

Dublin

WALES

Cromwell's army in 1649. His soldiers took a great deal more land in the rest of Ireland

Ireland

James II tried to get back his throne by attacking England's back door, Ireland. Most of Ireland was Catholic, and supported him. James's troops attacked Ulster, where English and Scots Protestant settlers had taken over the land.

James's Catholic troops began a siege of Londonderry, and fixed a big wooden beam across the harbour entrance so none of William's ships could bring supplies. Protestants in Londonderry were determined to hold out. They got so short of food that they ate dogs, rats and candles. In the end William's ships broke through, and the siege ended. Then William himself brought an army over, and defeated James at the Battle of the Boyne in 1690.

William took over the whole of Ireland. The English continued to try to control both religion and the land in Ireland. The Irish did not give in, and their hatred of England grew. There are still terrible problems in Ireland. Many of them began in the time covered by this book.

Problems in Ireland

A Religion
Irish Catholics could not:
- be lawyers, soldiers or MPs
- send their children to Catholic schools
- use church buildings – Protestants took them.

B Land
Percentage of the land owned by Irish Catholics:
1640: 59%
1658: 22%
1714: 7%

1 Draw three circles (pie charts), each representing 100 per cent, for the three dates in **B**. Mark in and colour the correct sized sector of each circle to represent land owned by Irish Catholics. Put a key to explain your chart.

2 Explain in your own words why by 1700:
a) Ulster wanted to be ruled by an English king
b) The rest of Ireland did not.

LEST WE FORGET.
1688. 1690.
WILLIAM III.

This is a modern picture of William III in Ireland. Protestants in Northern Ireland today use pictures of 'King Billy' to show they do not want to become part of the rest of Ireland. What do Protestants not want to forget? Why are the two dates there? How does the picture show they want to stay British?

Scotland

The flag on the right shows what happened in 1707 between England and Scotland. They at last agreed it would be sensible if they became one kingdom – **Britain**. England was fighting a long and bitter war with France. They could not risk having an enemy to the north as well. So they gave Scotland some of the things she wanted – better trade, her own church, law courts and schools. It was a bargain, which suited both sides fairly well. However, some Scots do not agree to this day.

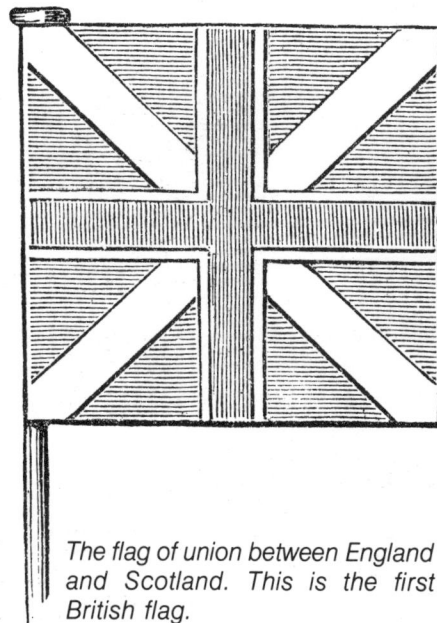

The flag of union between England and Scotland. This is the first British flag.

■ Copy the flag in colour. Find out why it has that design, and how it is different from today's Union Jack.

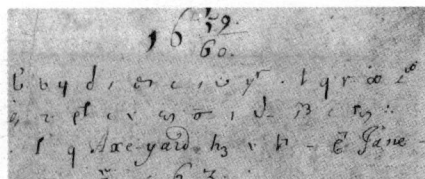

This is how Pepys's diary begins:
Blessed be God, at the end of the last year I was in very good health, without any *sense* [feeling] of my old pain but of taking of cold. I lived in Axe Yard, having my wife and servant Jane, and no more in the family but us three.

No one discovered Pepys's diary and learnt to read his shorthand until long after his death. He usually writes names in the ordinary way. You can probably pick them out.

Samuel Pepys and his times

On 1 January 1660 a young Londoner called Samuel Pepys began to keep a diary. He wrote it in a kind of shorthand so that other people could not read his secrets, and he kept it up for nine years. We are lucky Pepys kept his diary, because it tells us what it was like to live in Charles II's England. The information on these two pages all comes from his diary.

Pepys had a job in the Navy Office, organising supplies and pay. He worked very hard, and helped to improve the ships in the navy. He kept very careful accounts. He learnt his multiplication tables so that he could do the accounts properly.

Pepys was a lucky man. He had an operation to cut a stone as big as a tennis ball out of his gall-bladder, and survived it. ← 20 That is what he meant when he began his diary by saying he did not have his 'old pain' any more. Every year he had a special dinner to celebrate the anniversary of his operation. This is what Pepys and seven friends ate in 1663:

A fricassee of rabbits and chicken	A dish of four lobsters
A leg of mutton boiled	3 tarts
3 carps in a dish	A lamprey pie
A great dish of a side of lamb	A dish of anchovies
A dish of roasted pigeons	Good wine of several sorts

Pepys's wife Elizabeth prepared that meal with the help of their one servant Jane. It must have taken a lot of work. Washing clothes was hard work too. Once after Pepys had enjoyed a jolly evening drinking and singing, he says he wrote his diary and went to bed at 1 a.m., and his wife and the maid were still up, doing the washing.

Fashions

Pepys married Elizabeth when he was 22 and she was 15. He was fond of her. Once when they went to court, Pepys said she looked much prettier than the King's sister whose 'hair was frizzed up to her ears'. Elizabeth 'with two or three black patches and well dressed did seem much handsomer'. It was very fashionable to wear tiny round or star-shaped black patches on your face.

Pepys enjoyed fashionable clothes too, especially when he did well in his job, and began to go up in the world. Like most people then, he did not wash himself very much, and he often had lice in his hair. In the end he decided to have his hair cut off, and to buy a fashionable new wig. This cost him £3 (quite expensive – he paid his servant £4 a year). The wig-maker made him a second wig out of his own hair. When he went to church rather nervously wearing his new wig 'I thought all the church would have cast their eye all upon me – but I found no such thing.' He seems rather disappointed nobody noticed!

Samuel Pepys
- Born 1633
- Married Elizabeth 1655
- Operation 1658
- Began diary 1660
- Gave up diary 1669
- Worked in Navy Office until 1689
- Died 1703

Pepys and his wife quarrelled more as time went by. Once they came to blows, and he gave his wife a black eye. He was very embarrassed afterwards. Pepys was not a faithful husband either. He often flirted with barmaids, and later one of their own servants.

Houses and furniture

Pepys bought a bigger house in 1666 and had his own and his wife's portraits painted to go in the main room. The walls and furniture probably looked like the room in the picture on this page. Pepys had the walls specially painted. It cost him £83. You can see what houses looked like in Pepys's time on page 114.

Furniture was getting more comfortable. Chairs had padded seats and backs. The heavy curtains round the four-poster bed are not a new idea. People still did not believe in fresh air at night! What else can you see in the room? How would it be lit and heated?

The portrait that went in Pepys's new house in 1666 now hangs in the National Portrait Gallery in London. Pepys paid the artist, John Hayls, £14 for the painting, and 25s for the frame. Wigs at this time were quite natural looking. The picture shows another of Pepys's interests. He is holding a song he has composed. He often enjoyed musical evenings with his friends.

1. Make sketches with labels to show fashions for women and men in Pepys's time. Use these two pages and the pictures on pages 115 and 120-1. Look up other books if you can.

2. Fashionable men began to wear wigs about 1663. The fashion (in different styles) lasted for more than 100 years. Why do you think men liked wearing wigs?

3. Make sketches of furniture using the picture on this page. Copy out the meal on page 108. Use a dictionary, and explain what all the dishes are. Use your common sense, and write some sentences to explain why the washing was such a long job.

4. Write a paragraph about Pepys. Use these words to help you:
   diary   servant
   job   interests
   wife   character

Read pages 18–19 before you start these two pages. Remind yourself how plague spread. The regulations to try to stop plague, which were made in London in 1563, were used again in 1665. Read them carefully.

Plague, 1665

London in Pepys's time was the biggest city in western Europe. Nearly half a million people lived there. Houses were still mainly built of wood and plaster, with thatched roofs. Many of them had upstairs rooms which jutted out over the street, and were so close together that people could lean out of their bedroom windows and touch the house opposite. Streets were often dark and muddy, with a filthy open drain running down the middle. The poorest people lived in crowded slums full of tumble-down houses. These slums were mostly outside the old city walls, and along the main roads leading out of the city.

London was still a very dirty place. There was often a thick cloud over the city. People had smoky coal fires in their houses. Soap, beer, and dyes were made in London, and there were sugar-boiling sheds too. All these industries gave off dense fumes which polluted the atmosphere.

Rats and fleas were everywhere. There had been four bad outbreaks of plague since 1600. In 1665 came the worst epidemic of all. About a quarter of the people in London died. Pepys stayed in London all the time, and, luckily for him, did not catch it. He tells us what London was like then:

> *7 June:* The hottest day that ever I felt in my life. . . . This day . . . I did in Drury Lane see two or three houses marked with a red cross upon the doors, and 'Lord have mercy upon us' writ there – which was a sad sight . . . I was forced to buy some roll-tobacco to smell and chew.
> *12 July:* A solemn fast day for the plague growing upon us.
> *12 August:* The people die so, that now it seems they [must] carry the dead to be buried by daylight, the nights not sufficing to do it in.
> *20 September:* No boats upon the river; grass grows tall up and down Whitehall . . .
> *16 October:* But Lord how empty the streets are, . . . so many poor sick people in the streets, full of sores . . . in Westminster there is never a physician, and but one apothecary ←| 21 | left, all being dead.
> *22 November:* I heard this day the plague is come very low; that is 600 . . . and hopes of a further decrease because of . . . exceeding hard frost.

A

B

C

Multituds flying from London by water in boats & barges.

D

Flying by land.

E

Burying the dead with a bell before them.   Searchers.

F

Carts full of dead to bury.

Pictures drawn in 1665, showing scenes in London during the plague.

Figures of deaths from plague in London in 1665, taken from lists made at the time:

May	43	September	26 230
June	590	October	14 375
July	6137	November	3449
August	17 036	December	590

1 a) Make a block graph from the figures of plague deaths for each month. Use 1 cm for every 1000 deaths. Heading: Plague deaths in London in 1665.

    b) Which months sound the worst from Pepys's diary? Does your graph agree? Under the blocks in your graph, draw symbols to show what Pepys says about the weather. (Make sure you choose the right month.)

2 Why do you think the figure Pepys gives for plague deaths on 22 November is different from the November total on your graph? Why is it difficult to know exactly how many people died of the plague?

3 Look at Pepys's diary entry for 7 June. What was going on inside the houses with red crosses on the doors? How do you know?

4 How do you know from the diary that a lot of people left London?

5 Look carefully at the pictures **A–F**. Find the searchers and the door with a cross on it in **A**. Write down what all the people are doing in **B**. From what Pepys says, in which months do you think **C** and **D** took place? Are they rich or poor people who are escaping? Why is a bell used in **E**? Why are there no coffins in **F**?

6 Use the pictures to write a story about the London Plague of 1665.

7 Draw the picture of the doctor in the margin. Write labels to explain what he is wearing and holding, and how he thought this would protect him. How would you feel if you were a plague patient being treated by this doctor?

Some doctors wore a costume like this when they visited people with plague. The 'beak' was filled with perfume or herbs.

The Great Fire of London, 1666

This is not a picture of the fire of 1666, but it gives a good idea of how people tried to put out fires in towns, and the equipment they used.

At 3 o'clock on the morning of 2 September 1666, Mr Farriner, a London baker in Pudding Lane, had a nasty problem. He was busy baking the bread to sell that day when his oven caught fire. In no time his house was ablaze, and he and his family had to escape fast. The fire began to spread down the street.

At the same time that night, Pepys was fast asleep in bed. Suddenly the maid Jane ran in and woke him, saying there was a great fire in the city. Pepys got up to have a look. Fires happened quite often, and he decided this one was nothing very much. He went back to sleep.

When Pepys got up in the morning he soon realised this fire was serious. More than 300 houses were already burnt. The weather had been very dry, and a strong wind was fanning the flames. London Bridge was ablaze. People were trying desperately to save their belongings, and loading them into boats on the river.

King Charles II sent orders to pull down houses that were in the path of the fire, to try to stop it. Pepys met the Lord Mayor in a panic, 'like a fainting woman,' crying, 'Lord, what can I do? I am spent! People will not obey me. I have been pulling down houses. But the fire overtakes us faster than we can do it.'

Later the King and his brother James came themselves to help fight the fire. But nothing seemed to stop it. The pigeons often hovered too near the places where their nests had been, and were burnt. Pepys said that by the evening:

> with one's face in the wind, you were almost burned with a shower of firedrops ... we stayed till it being darkish, we saw the fire as one entire arch of fire ... above a mile long. It made me weep to see it. The churches, houses, and all on fire and flaming at once, and a horrid noise the flames made, and the cracking of houses at their ruin.

London burned for four terrible days. St Paul's Cathedral was in ruins. The fire destroyed 88 churches and 13 000 houses. One hundred thousand people had no homes. Pepys was lucky (as he had been during the Plague too). The flames got to the bottom of his street, but his house was not burnt, and nor was his office.

Surprisingly, not very many people died. A Catholic Frenchman called Robert Hubert was hanged a month later for starting the fire. But afterwards (too late for him) it became clear that he had not even been in England at the time.

The Fire of 1666 was the worst fire London had ever had. People soon began to call it the Great Fire of London.

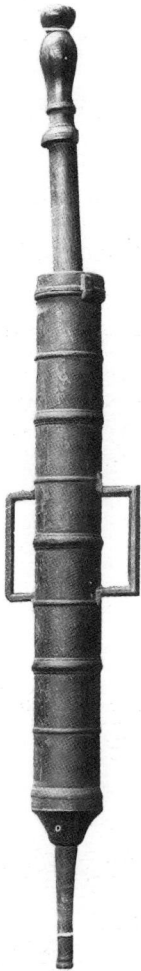

People also used hand pumps like this to fight fires. How useful do you think it was?

1 Draw all the fire-fighting equipment on this page. Label each drawing: explain how the equipment was used, and how useful you think it would have been. Then make a list of modern fire-fighting equipment, and point out some differences.

2 Find as many reasons as you can on these two pages why the Fire spread so quickly. (Use page 110 too.) ✎

3 Pepys wrote in his diary on 2 September that the fire started in the baker's house in Pudding Lane. A lot of other people must have known that too. So why do you think Robert Hubert was blamed? ✎

4 Write your own description of the Great Fire of London. ✎

The scene in London at the height of the Great Fire of 1666. You can see the houses and some of the spires of the 88 churches which were burnt. Find London Bridge, St Paul's Cathedral, and the Tower of London. Which one escaped the fire? ← 75

Did the Great Fire of London stop the plague coming back?

The plague never came back to London again after 1665. We are not sure why it died out. No one discovered how plague spread until 200 years later, so that was not the reason.

What about the rats? The black rats which carried the plague seem to have disappeared from Western Europe about this time. There were plenty of brown rats, but they did not carry plague. ← 18

People often say the Great Fire stopped London having plague. You can see some of the new stone and brick houses, which were built after the Fire, on the next page. They were cleaner, and better built. So there were fewer rats and fleas about.

■ Make your own copy of the map of London which shows where the Plague was worst, and how much of London was burnt in the Fire. ✎

■ Why do you think the Plague was worst in the shaded areas? ← 110 Write your answer under the map. ✎

■ Is the map evidence that the rebuilding of London after the Great Fire is the most important reason why plague never came back? Discuss this in class, and then write your opinion under the map. ✎

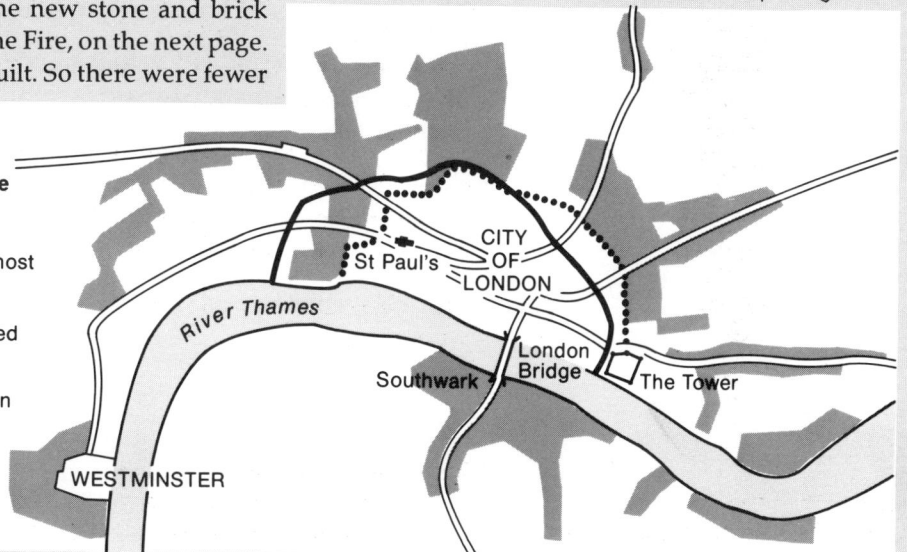

London during the Plague and Fire

Areas where there were most cases of plague in 1665

Boundary of area destroyed in the fire

•••••• Walls of the City of London

113

The rebuilding of London

Fish Street – London's new look. These four-storey houses were built of brick or stone, with big windows. They had tiled roofs instead of thatch. In the middle of the wide street is the Monument. It is 61.5 metres high, and built in memory of the Fire, near Pudding Lane where the Fire started. Christopher Wren was its main designer. (The words at the bottom still blamed the Catholics for starting it.) Further down the street is one of Wren's new churches. All his churches had different and beautiful spires.

The Great Fire of 1666 gave Londoners a wonderful chance to improve their city when they rebuilt it. They were lucky too. They had the right man to plan it for them.

Christopher Wren was an astronomer, and studied mathematics. He had just begun to design buildings as well. The Great Fire gave him his chance. He became the most famous English architect of all time. But he did not have an easy time. Five days after the Fire, he produced a plan which would have made London into a very beautiful city with wide streets and many open spaces. The trouble was that people whose houses had been burnt wanted to rebuild them in exactly the same spot. Nobody followed Wren's plan. London still had many narrow crowded streets.

Christopher Wren did a lot, all the same. He designed 51 new churches to replace the ones which were burnt. His greatest building is St Paul's Cathedral. Its huge dome towered over the new London. He designed it so well that it has lasted 300 years, and stood firm during the air-raids in the Second World War. Wren was buried in St Paul's. There is a Latin sentence on his tombstone. It means: 'If you want to see his monument, look around you.'

1 Find pictures of Wren's London churches, and make a class frieze of the towers, spires, and St Paul's dome.

2 Two questions to discuss with the class:
   a) If you were a London citizen trying to rebuild your shop after the Fire, what would you have thought of Wren's plan?
   b) Are we better at planning our cities now? (Find out first about new buildings, traffic problems, fire risks, in your area.)

New goods to buy

The Duchess of Portsmouth was one of Charles II's mistresses, and is dressed in the height of fashion. Her dress is blue silk, and under it she wears a 'shift' or under-dress of fine muslin cotton. The black slave girl wears these luxury materials too. What is she holding? The slave herself is there because of a profitable trade.

Coffee houses became fashionable meeting places for men in Charles II's reign. By 1700, there were over 2000 coffee houses like this one in London. Friends, business men and politicians met to chat, read the newspapers (which had just started), smoke pipes and drink coffee. Find the tobacco pipes, coffee bowls (no one used saucers yet) and a servant with a coffee pot.

The rich people in these pictures are using many new goods. People alive in the times at the beginning of this book might not have heard of some of them. If they had, they would be expensive and rare. In 1450, sugar was a great luxury. Rich people occasionally bought an expensive 'sugar loaf'. Poor people never tasted it at all. They used honey or nothing. By 1700 sugar was plentiful. People used it to sweeten the fashionable new drinks of coffee, tea and chocolate, which they drank out of delicate china bowls without handles. (These bowls came from China, which explains their name.)

There were new fruits and vegetables: pineapples, tomatoes and potatoes. Tobacco was cheap enough for quite poor people to buy. Pepys ate turkey, which was another new food.

Trade brought these goods into England. Many trading ships sailed up the Thames to London, making the city richer still. By 1700, England had become a great trading nation.

■ Make an illustrated list of all the goods mentioned on this page, including those in the pictures.

Slaves

When Europeans arrived in the New World of America, they wanted to make their fortunes. The Spanish found gold and silver mines. Later Spanish and English people began to grow sugar and tobacco in plantations (farms) in the Caribbean and North America. It was very hard work to produce these crops.

The Europeans had guns. They conquered the local people, and forced them to work in mines and plantations. It is a tragic fact that European wars, and European diseases, killed off many of these people. So the Europeans were short of people to work for them.

At the same time, on the other side of the Atlantic, Europeans were exploring the West African coast. First the Portuguese, and then the English in Elizabeth I's reign, found many different African peoples there. Local tribes already bought and sold prisoners in local wars as slaves. It was easy for Europeans to buy these slaves too. And they knew they could sell them in the Caribbean where Europeans wanted workers to produce sugar and tobacco.

This is how the slave trade grew. We find it horrifying now. Europeans then found the peoples of West Africa different and strange. They saw nothing wrong in treating slaves as if they were not human at all, and buying and selling them like animals. They made money out of it too, of course. This explains why they started the slave trade. But it does not make it any better.

Sir John Hawkins's crest. Sir John Hawkins was one of Elizabeth I's famous sailors. In 1562, he became the first Englishman to take slaves across the Atlantic from West Africa, to sell in the Caribbean. He did very well out of it, and was proud of his success. So he designed this new crest to display on his coat of arms (family badge), and saw nothing wrong in it.

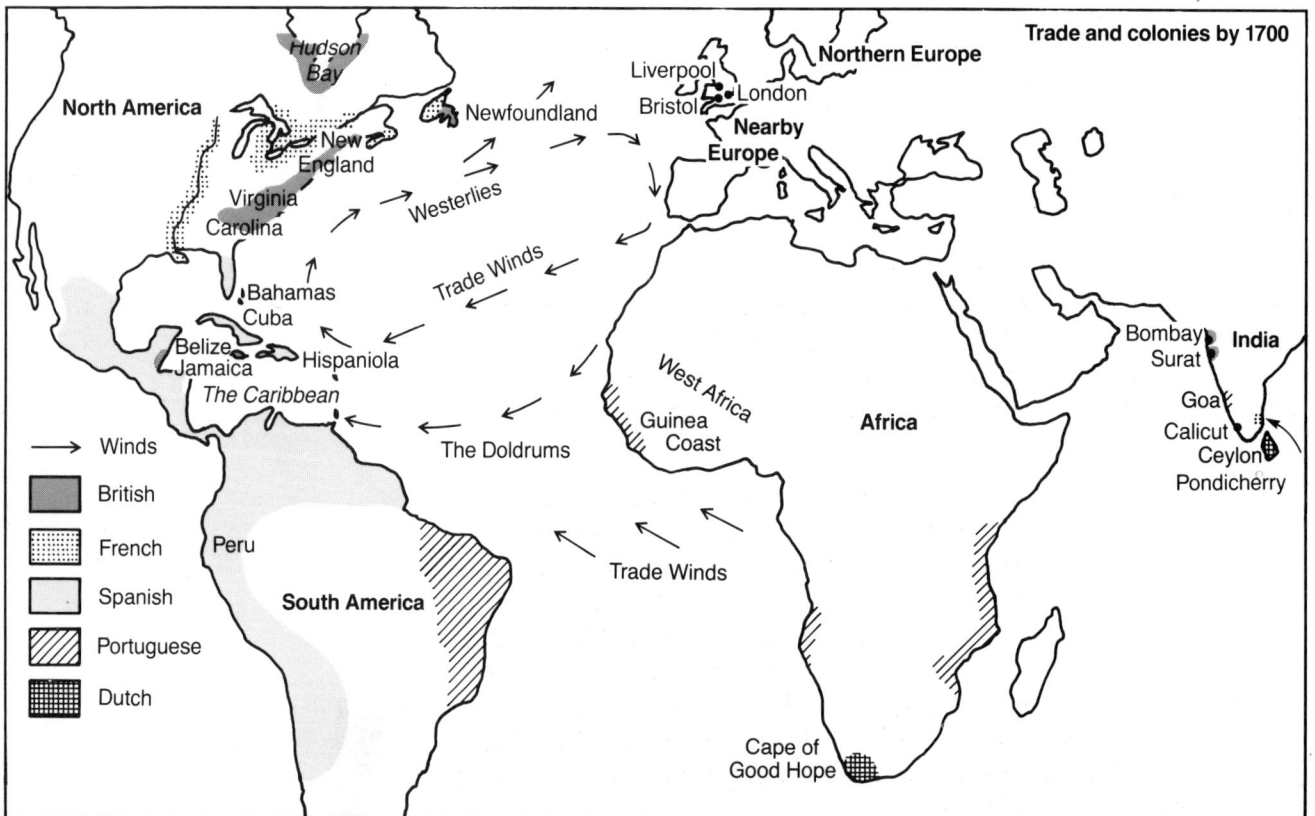

Trade and colonies by 1700

Hudson Bay

North America

Newfoundland

New England

Virginia
Carolina

Westerlies

Trade Winds

Bahamas
Cuba

Belize
Jamaica
Hispaniola
The Caribbean

The Doldrums

Northern Europe

Liverpool
Bristol
London

Nearby Europe

West Africa

Guinea Coast

Africa

Bombay
Surat

India

Goa
Calicut
Ceylon
Pondicherry

Winds

British

French

Spanish

Portuguese

Dutch

Peru

South America

Trade Winds

Cape of
Good Hope

The triangle

By the middle of the seventeenth century, the slave trade worked like a triangle.

Side 1   An English ship sailed from London or Bristol to West Africa, loaded with cheap cloth, beads and guns. On the West African coast, they exchanged the cargo they had brought for slaves. They crammed as many slaves as they could on to the lower decks of the ship in horrible conditions.

Side 2   The journey across the Atlantic to the Caribbean took about six weeks. There, the cargoes of these ships changed again. The slaves who had lived through the journey were sold, mainly to sugar plantation owners. They worked cutting the tough sugar cane, and in the hot sugar-boiling sheds. Some worked as house servants. Some made another journey – to North America to produce tobacco and later cotton. Some came to England, like the girl in the picture on page 115.

Side 3   Now the ship loaded up with sugar, rum, molasses (all sugar products) and tobacco. When the ship got back to England the ship owners sold their cargo. They made a lot of money.

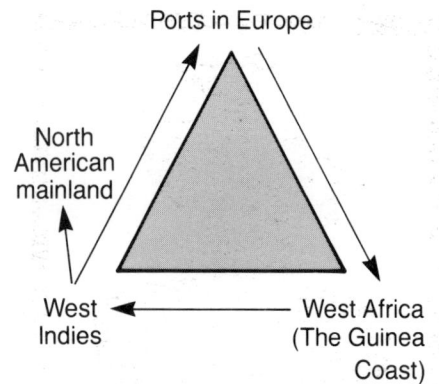

The slave trade triangle

1 On your copy of the map opposite, draw in the slave triangle, and neatly write in the cargoes on each side of the triangle.

2 How did wind help trade between England and the Caribbean?

3 Explain in your own words how these facts led to the slave trade growing fast from about 1650 onwards:
- The new habit of putting sugar in the fashionable drinks of tea, coffee and chocolate.
- The Europeans who owned the sugar plantations in the Caribbean made a lot of money selling sugar.
- Sugar production needed many workers.

The East

In 1583, a merchant called Ralph Fitch set out from London to explore the East and to trade there. He went with other merchants, and they carried a special letter from Queen Elizabeth I. It was written to Akbar, the Mughal Emperor of Muslim India. It asked Akbar to treat the merchants kindly and to allow them to trade.

Akbar ruled over lands bigger than the whole of Europe. He was a great soldier and builder, and had many other interests. When Ralph Fitch reached Akbar's lands after many adventures, he was very impressed. He found cities bigger and more beautiful than London. And he realised how many luxury goods like silks, cotton, dyes and jewels could be sold in England. Fitch travelled as far as Burma before he returned home. When he did, he set all London talking with the wonders he had seen in the East. In 1600, Queen Elizabeth founded the East India Company to trade with the East, and especially India.

This is a picture of Jahangir, Akbar's son, who became the next Mughal Emperor. His great power is shown by the double halo round him. It is so bright that the little cherubs above him shield their eyes.

But the picture has another message. Jahangir is sitting on an hour glass, and the sands are running out. He is looking at a holy Muslim teacher and giving him a book. He is not taking much notice of two important rulers who are also in the picture – the Sultan of Turkey and James I of England. (Though we know he was friendly towards both of them.)

The Indian artist who has painted his picture has put himself in at the bottom left-hand corner. He must have seen western pictures. He knows what James I looked like (compare with the portrait on page 80), and his cherubs look rather like western pictures too. But he does not mind about not using western ideas of space and distance in a picture. The beautiful patterned carpet makes a wonderful background, and almost looks as if it is hanging straight down, instead of being flat on the ground.

We know that James I's ambassador, Sir Thomas Roe, visited Jahangir and gave him presents. Perhaps one of them was a portrait of James. He wrote:

I went to the Court at four in the evening, to the Durbar, which is the Place where the Mughal sits out daily, to entertain strangers, to receive petitions and presents, to give commands, to see, and to be seen . . . The King sits in a little gallery overhead . . . covered with canopies of velvet and silk, underfoot laid with good carpets . . . I delivered his Majesty's letter translated . . . my presents were well received . . . He dismissed me with more favour and grace . . . than was ever shown to any ambassador.

It was an important visit because Jahangir gave the East India Company permission to have a base at Surat, and trade in silks, cotton (calico and muslin), indigo (a dye) and saltpetre (used in gunpowder). From then on, India became more and more important to England.

1 What are the two messages Jahangir wants his picture to give?

2 How is this picture evidence that English people must have visited his court? (*Clue* We know Jahangir and his artist never travelled to Europe.)

3 Was Sir Thomas Roe pleased with his visit to Jahangir's court? Explain your answer.

4 Find out more about Akbar and his court. Try to read *Elizabeth and Akbar* by Annabel Wigner (Stanley Thornes, 1987).

An important day in Tichborne

On the next page, there is a picture of people living in the times you have been reading about in this chapter. It is an important day (it happens every year) in a small village in Hampshire called Tichborne. The squire, who lives in the big house and owns all the land round about, is giving out a dole (gift) of bread to the poor in the village. This year (1670) he is paying an artist to paint a picture showing the event.

Find the **squire**. He is standing in front, slightly to the left and very much in control. He has a big white collar and dark coat. His children stand by him. Can you see the two village children staring at them?

The squire is holding his teenage daughter's hand. Her dress has a bodice stiffened with bones or strips of wood, and a skirt with many layers of material. She must stand straight and not run about much. She is probably learning French, dancing, embroidery and how to behave in polite society. Then she will be ready to marry. She will have to be very strong-minded if she wants to do anything else. How different is her life from a rich girl's in Chapter 1?

Now find a **rich family from London**. They are relations or friends of the squire, and are in the middle of the picture. They are dressed very fashionably. The man has a wig, and a lace cravat round his neck instead of a collar. Like some of the other people in the picture, this man is enjoying most of the changes you have read about in this chapter.

The **house servants** stand behind the squire on the left of the picture. They hold baskets of bread for the villagers. One of them is black, so he has probably come to England on a slave ship. They are all quite well dressed – some may be less important family relations. The servants do not go short of food, but they do not have much freedom either. They must please the squire, or lose their jobs.

The **villagers** wait on the right of the picture to receive their dole. An old man is shuffling forward. We do not know what they all feel about their dole. Perhaps they are just glad to have some help. The squire controls their lives too. He employs most of them. They live in houses which belong to him and pay him rent.

Life has not changed much for these ordinary people. Food, work, tools, enjoyment, illness – they are much the same for them as for the ordinary people you read about in Chapter 1. Many of them cannot read or write. If there is a bad harvest, they will go hungry. They could be in the picture on page 4 of this book, as well as in the last picture.

We have seen some great changes in our place in time. But a lot has not changed. History is like that.

Changing times
- A new King and Queen, with less power
- More trade
- New goods
- New drinks
- More stone and brick houses
- No more plague (but still many other diseases)
- New ideas in science:
  The Royal Society founded by Charles II in 1660 to study science
  William Harvey (1578–1657) discovered the circulation of the blood – but few people believed him
  Isaac Newton (1642–1727) discovered the force of gravity and studied light
  Edmund Halley (1656–1742), astronomer, discovered the path of 'Halley's comet'

The Tichborne Dole *by Gilles von Tillborch 1670*

■ Choose three people in the picture:
- someone who would know about and enjoy most of the changes in the list on page 119 – probably all of them.
- someone who would have met some of the changes
- someone who is hardly affected by the changes at all.

Draw them, and write underneath your reasons for choosing them.

Key words in this section to help you remember and understand what you have learnt. You should be able to use these words now and find evidence in the chapter which illustrates each of them.

Revolution
heir
Catholic
Protestant
Bill of Rights

Ireland
siege
battle
religion
land

Scotland
bargain
union
flag

Samuel Pepys
diary
operation
food
fashions
wigs

Plague
bacteria
rat
flea
regulations
epidemic

Fire
fire-fighting
pump
destruction

Rebuilding
astronomer
mathematics
architect
design
dome
spire
tower
The Monument

Trade
goods
luxuries
profit
slaves
plantations
ambassador
silk
cotton
indigo
saltpetre

Science
Royal Society
circulation of the blood
gravity
light
astronomer
comet

Tichborne
dole
squire
servants
villagers

Acknowledgements

The author and publishers are grateful to the following for permission to reproduce material.

Ashmolean Museum, Oxford, pages 71 (bottom), 92, 100 (top) • Biblioteca Ambrosiana, Milan, page 24(A) • British Library, pages 15 (top left and bottom right), 36 (right), 50 (top), 75, 86, 94 (top), 97, 98 (right) • Board of Trustees of the Victoria and Albert Museum, London, pages 11 (bottom), 53 (top centre), 68 (left), 99 • Bodleian Library, Oxford, page 71 (signature) • College of Arms, page 40 • *Country Life*/IPC Magazines, page 63 (bottom) • Dean and Chapter, Hereford Cathedral, page 27 • Dean and Chapter, Westminster Abbey, page 38 (top) • English Heritage, page 51 • Freer Gallery of Art, Smithsonian Institution, Washington DC, page 118 • Guildhall Library, London, pages 74, 76 (top left) • Hulton Picture Company, pages 3, 12, 31 (left), 63 (top), 90, 95 (bottom), 103 (right) • John Freeman and Co., pages 52, 62 (bottom), 76 (bottom left and bottom right), 87 (left) • Mansell Collection, pages 8 (bottom), 9 (bottom), 15 (top right), 21, 30 (bottom), 57, 72, 78, 81 (bottom), 101 (right), 107 (right), 112 (top), 113, 115 (right) • Marquess of Bath, Longleat House, Warminster, Wilts, page 10 • Marquess of Salisbury/John Freeman & Co., page 4 • Marquess of Tavistock and the Trustees of the Bedford Estates, page 68 (right) • Mary Evans Picture Library, pages 11 (top), 20 (top right, bottom left and bottom right), 26 (top), 53 (bottom), 76 (top right) • Mary Rose Trust, pages 1, 42 (left), 43 • Master and Fellows, Magdalene College, Cambridge, pages 42 (right), 108, 109 (bottom), 111 (C, D, E and F) • Musées Royaux des Beaux-Arts, Brussels, page 14 • Museo del Prado, Madrid/Mas, Barcelona, page 55 • Museum of London/John Freeman & Co., pages 77 (top), 110 (A and B), 112 (bottom), 114 • National Gallery, London, pages 23, 85 • National Library of Scotland, page 44 • National Maritime Museum, London, pages 26 (bottom), 28, 65 (top left and right), 67 • National Portrait Gallery, London, cover illustration and pages (i), 34, 35, 37 (top), 39, 46, 47, 48, 53 (top right), 54, 62 (top), 64, 70, 71 (top), 80, 81 (top left and top right), 87 (right), 88 (top), 98 (top), 100 (right), 101 (left), 109 (top), 115 (left) • National Trust Photographic Library, page 73 (left and top right) • Öffentliche Kunstsammlung, Basel, page 49 • Plimoth Plantation Inc., Plymouth, Massachusetts, page 82 • Robert Ashby, page 107 (left) • Royal Commission on Historical Monuments, page 22 • Sir Ralph Verney, page 91 • Society of Antiquaries of London, page 37 (bottom) • Stadtbibliothek, Bern, page 32 (bottom right • State Library, Boston, Massachusetts, page 83 (A, E and F) • Sudeley Castle, Winchcombe, Glos, page 59 • Trustees of the British Museum, pages 24 (top, B and C), 25 (top), 32 (left), 58 (bottom), 60, 89, 103 • Wayland (Publishers) Ltd, page 13 • Wellcome Institute Library, London, page 111 (bottom) • York Castle Museum, page 95 (top) • York Department of Tourism, page 17.

The paintings on pages 67 and 120–1 are in private collections.

We acknowledge permission to reproduce the following © Crown material:

pages 38 (bottom; E101/413/2/2) and 61 (SP52/13 No. 1), © Crown material in the Public Record Office, reproduced with the permission of the Controller of Her Majesty's Stationery Office.
Page 40 (left), © Crown reproduced with the permission of the Board of Trustees of the Royal Armouries, HM Tower of London.
Page 53 (top left), Windsor Castle, Royal Library © Crown 1989 Her Majesty the Queen.
Page 58 (top), reproduced by gracious permission of Her Majesty the Queen (Royal Collection).

Every effort has been made to contact copyright holders and we apologise if any have been overlooked.

Index